ON THE WINGS OF LOVE

ON THE WINGS OF LOVE

Georgian Elopement Stories

NAOMI CLIFFORD

Joanne Major and Sarah Murden

978-1-9196232-4-5

A CIP record for this book is available from the British Library.

Caret Press
9 Durand Gardens, London SW9 0PS
info@caretpress.com caretpress.com

NAOMI CLIFFORD is an acclaimed author and history writer. She is a co-host of The Door history podcast, co-editor of Vauxhall History website and chairman of Friends of Stockwell War Memorial and Gardens.

Naomi studied history at Bristol University and, after a career in magazine journalism and production, returned to her first love: history, especially the history of women on the margins. Her published works include *The Disappearance of Maria Glenn* (2016), which looks at the fate of a sixteen-year-old girl who was abducted from her home in 1817; *Women and the Gallows 1797-1837: Unfortunate Wretches*, an exploration of the stories of women hanged in England and Wales; and *The Murder of Mary Ashford*, which recounts the case of a young woman whose rape and murder in Birmingham remains controversial. *Under Fire* (2021), which uses the diaries of a volunteer ambulance driver to tell the story of the London Blitz, has been praised as 'one of the best descriptive accounts of the World War Two bombing of Chelsea and London'. *Out of the Shadows*, a collection of Naomi's essays on a selection of 18th and 19th-century women, was published by Caret Press in 2022.

CONTRIBUTORS

JOANNE MAJOR is the author of several historical non-fiction works published by Pen & Sword Books, including *Kitty Fisher: The First Female Celebrity* (2023). She lives in Lincolnshire and is studying for an MA in Creative Writing at the University of Lincoln. Joanne's website is www.joannemajor.com, and a full list of her books can be found at www.pen-and-sword.co.uk.

SARAH MURDEN, FRHistS, is an historian of the eighteenth century who focuses on the lives of women. She hosts the popular website All Things Georgian, which looks at aspects of the Georgian era. Sarah also co-authored with Joanne Major *All Things Georgian: Tales from the Long Eighteenth Century* as well as four biographies, all of which are published by Pen & Sword Books.

CONTENTS

INTRODUCTION

RUNAWAY AND SECRET marriage has always existed — you only need think of the tragic story of Peter Abelard and Héloïse Argenteuil in twelfth-century France or the fictional plot of *Romeo and Juliet.* In the Georgian era, there was a new dimension to clandestine marriage — *elopement*, a term that developed into a cultural trope that captured the public imagination.

But what does the word *elopement* mean? In the twenty-first century it suggests a wedding conducted abroad, possibly on a distant island, to which only a handful of family and friends are invited, the aim being to avoid a dismal day under a marquee. Perhaps this is closer to its core meaning, *the act of running away.*[1]

Until the mid-eighteenth century the primary use of the verb *to elope* was *to abscond*, action usually undertaken in circumstances of bondage or threat. Servants, slaves and spouses eloped from their responsibilities and obligations and ships were named *The Elope* to celebrate their skills in dodging an enemy at sea. The preposition most often used with *elope* was *from*. As the century progressed, *elope* acquired an additional and narrower meaning, and a new preposition — *with* — and was employed in the context of an unmarried woman, often a minor, leaving home surreptitiously in order to marry without the permission or approval of one or other parent or guardian.

Why did elopement become a phenomenon in the Georgian era? Before changes to the law in the mid-eighteenth century clandestine marriages could be carried out in any parish, away from the objections of family and friends; banns read out in church giving prior notice of the union were not required. A woman's possessions (and also, incidentally, her debts) passed to her husband on marriage, making unmarried women in possession of, or expecting, a fortune an obvious target for predatory men. There were ways to protect assets through trusts and the Court of Chancery for example, but if there was a gap between the death of a benefactor and those measures coming into force, a woman would become especially vulnerable.

The abduction of an heiress for forcible marriage had to be carried out with some care. Two examples from the period preceding the Georgian era showed how things could go seriously wrong for perpetrators. In a 1685 case, fourteen-year-old heiress Lucy Ramsay, who had a fortune of £5,000, was inveigled out of a coach in Hyde Park in London by people employed by John Brown and carried off to Brown's lodgings in the Strand. The following day Lucy was made to marry Brown under the threat that she would be taken to France, beyond the reach of her friends and with little hope of rescue. Brown was executed for his crime.

In 1701 seventeen-year-old heiress Pleasant Rawlins was arrested for a £200 debt. The charge had been fabricated by Haagen Swendsen, a German adventurer who had previously tried, and failed, to woo her. She was taken to the Star and Garter in Drury Lane, and then to The Vine in Holborn, where Swendsen's accomplice, Mrs Baynton, warned her that she would end up in Newgate prison unless she agreed to the marriage. By now more in fear of being murdered by her captors than of Newgate, Pleasant relented. At the subsequent trial Baynton 'pleaded her belly' (she was pregnant, which meant that she could not be executed) and was later reprieved from her death sentence, but Swendsen was hanged. Neither Pleasant Rawlins nor Lucy Ramsay had given their consent freely, so the courts viewed them as unmarried and therefore qualified, under the law, to testify against their abductors.[2]

The parson who married Pleasant Rawlins resided in the Fleet, a debtors' prison off what is now Farringdon Street, one of a number of locations in London where marriages could be conducted quickly and in secret. Some of the Fleet's clergy were defrocked or otherwise disgraced and could be relied on, for an appropriate reward, to look in the other direction if one or other of the parties was under coercion or incapable through drink or was a repeat customer.

After the Fleet was banned from holding marriages, the business moved to the area known as the Rules, a defined set of streets around the prison where privileged inmates, for a fee, were allowed to roam or lodge and which fell outside the jurisdiction of the church. Here the inns and coffee houses touted for customers. Such 'marriage houses' proved so popular that it has been estimated that half the unions in London took place in one.

Clandestine marriage could have serious effects on lives, particularly those of women who married under duress. *The Derby Mercury* reported in 1721 that when Mrs Tuberville, 'a young Gentlewoman of a good fortune', was asked during an appearance at the Court of King's Bench whether she wanted to live with her husband or her guardians chose the latter. The Court ordered 'the Validity of the Marriage to be try'd before the Lord Chancellor' and sent her home with a tipstaff to ensure 'no Violence might be offer'd by her suppos'd Husband'.[3]

The problem of clandestine marriage was recognised long before Lord Hardwicke's Marriage Act (officially An Act for the Better Preventing of Clandestine Marriage) came into effect in England and Wales in 1754. Almost twenty years previously, *The Ipswich Journal* anticipated 'that a Bill will be brought into Parliament at the ensuing Sessions, to prevent the clandestine Marriages in the Fleet, which are now, and have been, for many Years past, transacted to the utter Ruin and Destruction of many Persons in this Kingdom, and is such a growing Evil, that 'tis thought high Time to be suppress'd; which the enlarging of the Rules of the Prison will hardly do.'[4]

Hardwicke's Act brought in stricter regulation of the conduct of the marriage ceremony. There were now only two routes to legal union, both requiring a four-week waiting period. Couples could either request the reading of banns in church for three Sundays in a row before the ceremony or, if marrying outside their parish, they could do so by licence, which meant registering with a member of the clergy and signing a bond to swear that at least one party to the marriage had lived in the parish for at least four weeks. Couples of all faiths, including Catholics and Nonconformists, had to be married by an Anglican minister, with Quaker and Jewish marriages the only exceptions.

Was Harwicke's law universally welcomed? No. What might look like a straightforward attempt to protect women from the predations of fortune-hunters and to impose regulation on a sphere rife with corruption was denounced in the House of Commons as a plot to 'secure all the rich heiresses in the kingdom for the aristocracy'.[5] At a time of changing attitudes to rank and of greater social mobility, some saw clandestine marriage as an acceptable form of levelling up. A lower-ranking man should be cheered on in his pursuit of a higher-class woman, not prosecuted or incarcerated for it. He was, after all, merely looking out for himself. Heiresses were prizes; any man would snare one if he had the chance.

One way to bypass the requirements of Lord Harwicke's Act was to lie to the clergyman about residence or age. It was illegal to marry an 'infant', that is someone over sixteen but under twenty-one, without the consent of their parents or guardian. Although the Act brought in strict punishments for priests who knowingly solemnised illegal marriages (they were liable to transportation for fourteen years) prosecutions were rare. Still, a failure to read the banns or obtain the appropriate sworn statements for the licence caused clergymen anxiety. In 1768 a curate in Berkshire who had married 'a young lady of immense fortune' to her father's groom without licence or publication of banns ran off from his place to avoid being sent to the colonies.[6] In 1809 comedy actor John Giles and underage heiress and ward of Chancery Augusta Nicholson, succeeded in having the banns read twice at St. Marylebone Church in London but were intercepted by Augusta's family before a marriage could take place (see Chapter 5). The clergyman was called in to the Lord Chancellor's chambers to explain why he had not made the appropriate checks on Miss Nicholson himself.[7]

Another way to circumvent the Act was to make for the most convenient region where English law did not apply — Ireland, the Isle of Man, the Channel Islands, France, or most usually Scotland, where the age of consent to marry was twelve for girls and fourteen for boys, with no caveat for parental consent. Some couples chose initially to go to ground in their nearest city, waiting for the hue and cry to abate before making the journey; others immediately sped north, hoping that their horses were faster than those of the pursuing families or their agents. Once on the road (often the Great North Road), perhaps with a maid in tow to preserve the reputation of the bride-to-be, the aim was to cross the border and marry as soon as possible. Gretna Green, two miles

FIG.1 Satirical print showing a clergyman marrying a young sailor and his landlady's daughter in the Fleet Market, engraved by John June (1747). *From Robert Chambers, Book of Days (1864)*

into Scotland, was not the only destination. Lamberton Toll, north of Berwick, and Coldstream were more convenient for travellers from Newcastle-on-Tyne and, if incensed parents or guardians were closing in, the tollkeeper at Sark Toll Bar, which was a mere step across the border, could perform the ceremony.

In the years immediately after the passing of Hardwicke's Act, few couples took the decision to flee, possibly because the roads were hazardous and the journey required a daunting level of planning. It was also expensive – £100 minimum, to include fees for the parson, overnight stops, food, horse chaises and a chaperone – as well as risky. As Richard Vining Perry and others found (see Chapter 1), prosecution and prison, as well as execution if found guilty of rape, were real possibilities. However, with the introduction of turnpikes to pay for improvements in the roads and the expansion of coaching services, the route became easier and faster to navigate. The chance of harsh sentences in the courts was also seen to reduce or became at least surmountable. Stolen brides rarely testified against their husbands – to do so would not only destroy their reputation but also render their children illegitimate.

Even if their families caught up with them before they reached Scotland or wherever they were trying for, eloping women were already compromised, particularly if they had spent a night alone with a man. In some families, a daughter was regarded as a commodity for trade. Some of the reputational damage to her unmarried siblings could be clawed back if she emerged from elopement legitimately married, and for this reason, many parents decided to cut their losses and insist that the runaway couple, once returned from their 'jaunt', marry again as soon as possible in the Established church.

MY HOPE, WHEN compiling the first fourteen chapters of this book and was that together they would show the wide compass of what could be called an elopement story, spanning Charles Baseley's grooming and stalking of Ann Wade, the fixation of Jemima Neate on the hapless Arthur Annesley Powell, to the flight of the Ladies of Llangollen from family disapproval to the touching attachment of Augusta Nicholson to John Giles.

The final chapter is a chronological selection of reports extracted

FIG.2 Filial affection, or, A trip to Gretna Green by Thomas Rowlandson (1785). An eloping couple drive headlong in a coach and four pursued by an irate father on horseback. A signpost points to Gretna Green. *Beinecke Rare Book and Manuscript Library*

from newspapers published in Britain and its empire between 1758 and 1837. My aim here was not to provide a comprehensive directory but to illustrate the range of scenarios that can be thought of as elopements and bride abductions as well as the strategies used by the protagonists and the reactions of their parents and friends. I have purposely not included any of the thousands of instances of elopement of *married* people because those involved issues, emotional, psychological and legal, of an altogether different stripe. It is worth remembering that stories appearing in newspapers represent only a fraction of elopements. Most families tried their utmost to protect their names and keep the details of their humiliation out of the public sphere.

Can the details of these newspaper stories be verified? In many cases, no. Newspapers were (and are) notoriously unreliable sources and often it is only when digging beneath the surface of individual cases that some of the truth emerges. To take one example, the reported elopement in 1817 of the sixteen-year-old girl whose experiences I researched for my book *The Disappearance of Maria Glenn* (see page 180) was described in the *Taunton Courier* in a deliberately misleading way: 'The lady professes the most enthusiastic and inviolable attachment to the object of her choice,' claimed the writer, neglecting to mention that a brother-in-law of the 'object' worked for the paper (and possibly was himself the author of the article) and that many of his in-laws and their associates were directly involved in Maria's removal from her home under cover of darkness.

Some journalists were themselves cynical about the veracity of the stories they published. An aside at the foot of an article republished in an Irish newspaper in 1837 put it succinctly: 'This has very much the air of "a cock-and-bull" story' (page 216). Apocryphal and probably fictitious stories about elopement were repeated sometimes at intervals of years, presumably as fillers on slow news days. I learned to be wary of reports that included beautifully composed but anonymous letters of apology or explanation from an eloper to a parent. The example published in the *Bath Chronicle* on 9 November 1769 was typical (see page 101).

What the newspaper stories demonstrate vividly is the tone employed by the journalists, who were, we can safely assume, all or nearly all men. Here there was a huge variety, from commiseration with distraught and furious parents to lascivious speculation on the intentions of the bridegroom. All the elements of what we now call tabloid journalism were present: obsession with celebrity, especially the rich (although the poor were also objects of interest, usually because they were aping their social betters by jumping on the elopement bandwagon); false concern for the victims; and downright lies. Much of the language was knowing and arch, replete with sexual innuendo: 'the matrimonial blacksmith' at Gretna was constantly 'hammering brides into wedlock on the reverend anvil', young ladies descended trees that raise their 'lusty branches'. Marked differences between the protagonists were especially titillating, which meant that stories of Jews eloping with gentiles, white women eloping with black men, and the very old with the very young always made good copy. There were elements of comedy. Ladders broke while the 'hero' descended with the 'fair fugitive' over his shoulder and couples argued on the journey and split up.

As the eighteenth century progressed, elopement became a widely understood cultural trope and featured in paintings, prints, novels, plays, songs, even in board games[8] and ceramics. Thomas Rowlandson's famous 1792 print (page 21) in which a scantily clad and nubile teenager lowers herself onto the shoulders of a dashing red-coated soldier who peers eagerly up her diaphanous dress illustrates a fascination with the sexual and financial possibilities of young boarding-school girls fired up with love. Feeding this were prurient assumptions about the sexual tastes of genteel young girls for what some might now disparagingly call 'a bit of rough'. Richard Brinsley Sheridan, himself an eloper and the subject of one of the essays in this book (see Chapter 13), used this theme in his 1775 play *The Rivals*, in which Lydia Languish, a beautiful young heiress, is determined to marry beneath her, for reasons of romance. In order to woo her, Captain Jack Absolute poses as a lowly ensign.

These newspaper stories, published to warn, entertain and reassure, were stuffed with cruel deceptions, jealous and violent fathers, disappointed and fretful mothers, assault, racism, snobbery and coercive control. There were some apparently happy outcomes, with reconciled families and satisfying financial settlements but the journalists were most excited by drama: thwarted obsessions ending in suicide and murder, reputations permanently destroyed and family bonds broken.

In Britain elopement continued well into the nineteenth century but gradually dropped out of favour. One reason was that new sensibilities around respectability and personal conduct regarded Gretna Green weddings, conducted in haste and in secret, as disgraceful. Another factor was the introduction of legal impediments to fugitive marriage, which included Lord Brougham's 'Cooling Off' Act of 1856 requiring one person in the couple to reside for twenty-one days in the parish where they wished to marry. It is interesting that as a young man Brougham had himself run away to marry in Scotland and that the union, although longlasting, proved to be unhappy. However, the prime reason for the decline was the Married Women's Property Acts, of 1870, which allowed married women to be the legal owners of the money they earned and to inherit property, and of 1882, which gave them the right to own and control property in their own right. By the turn of the twentieth century elopement became a subject of nostalgia, its darker sides forgotten in favour of a sugary gloss of ardent suitors and the triumph of love over parental opposition.

NAOMI CLIFFORD

ONE

THE BRISTOL ELOPEMENT

CLEMENTINA CLARKE & RICHARD VINING PERRY

The trial of Mr. Richard Vining Perry, indicted for feloniously taking away, marrying, &c. Miss Clementina Clarke (a young lady entitled to a fortune supposed to be ten thousand pounds per annum) came on to be tried before [Vicary] Gibbs, Esq. the Recorder of Bristol, and a common Jury, on the 14th. inst.

Derby Mercury, 24 April 1794

ALTHOUGH THIS TALE is about the ownership of a fortune made from chattel slavery rather than the process of amassing it, the origin of the riches Clementina Clarke[9] inherited as a teenager provokes in me the question: Why should we care about what happened to her? After all, although she was legally entitled to this money, ethically she was not. We have no reason to think that she, or anyone else closely involved in the plot against her, was in the least troubled by the philosophical and moral issues involved in its acquisition.

Of course we should exercise care when bringing twenty-first-century perspectives to bear on an eighteenth-century tale, although, in reality, we can have no other way of looking at it. My feeling is that, whatever the nature of the 'property' at the heart of this case, we should view Clementina as a manipulated and powerless child, locked into an abusive relationship with her husband. Her story provides a tragic example of many of the themes involved in the business of elopement and abduction for forcible marriage.

The relevant action began in 1791 when fourteen-year-old Clementina arrived at a small boarding-school in Park Street, Bristol run by sisters Mary and Selina Mills, who had purchased it from Hannah More, the renowned Evangelical educationist.[10] Clementina's immediate family was not wealthy — her Scottish father was a shoemaker in Banffshire — but her maternal uncle, George Ogilvie, had made a fortune from sugar estates in Jamaica. Ironically, just before Ogilvie died on 23 January 1791 he disinherited Clementina's brother, also named George, for marrying clandestinely, and left his portion to Clementina instead.

Not long after Ogilvie died, Richard Vining Perry,[11] a 26-year-old Bristol apothecary on the lookout for an easy way to make his fortune, spotted Clementina and some of her school friends walking on the Bristol Downs. According to his later account, he and Clementina fell madly and instantly in love. He described the moment it happened:

> As if the God of Nature by an exercise of a particular providence had directed their steps contrary to its general and immutable laws, their [that is, his and Clementina's] eyes met in attraction, and with a kind of electrical fire shook them to their souls.[12]

Perry did not mention Clementina's extremely attractive new fortune in his account nor that he had recently overheard her guardian, Mr. Gordon, talking loudly in a Bristol public house about Clementina and how her inheritance was not yet protected by the Court of Chancery.

Perry quickly formulated a plan. First he befriended a servant working in the boarding-school. Next, he sent the Mills sisters a note purporting to be from Mr. Gordon and inviting Clementina to tea with her aunt, Mrs. Ogilvie, in Clifton.[13] Then he decked out a carriage and horses in livery resembling that used by Mr. Gordon and sent it to fetch her. Selina Mills said later in court that Clementina, feeling low after the recent death of her father, had asked her teachers to come with her. Unfortunately, the Mills sisters both declined, and they thereby altered the course of their young pupil's life irrevocably. The carriage took her in the opposite direction to Clifton, to Perry's lodgings in Stokes Croft.

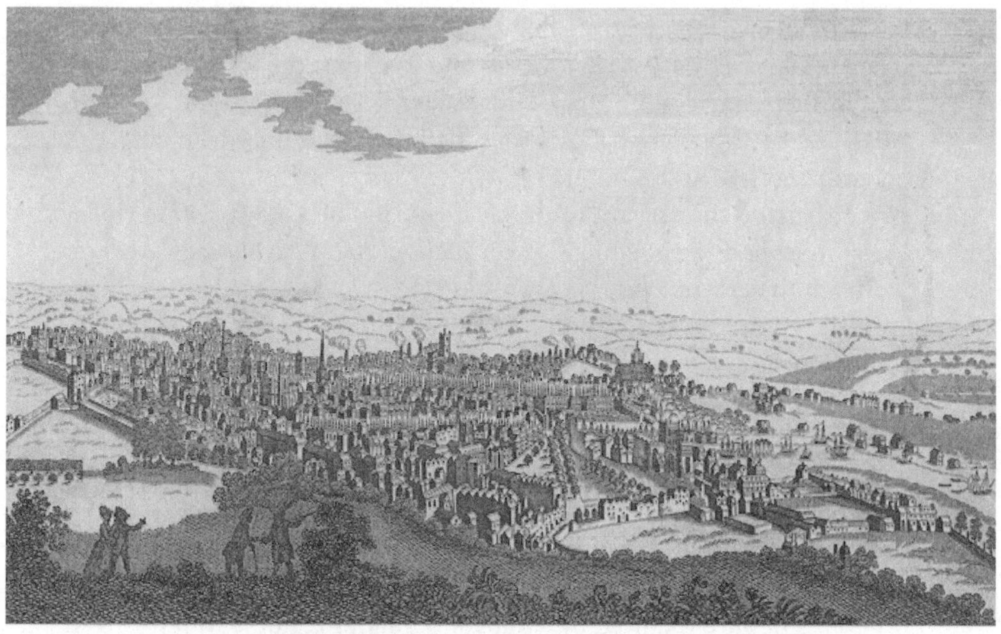

FIG.3 Perspective view of the city of Bristol, in the counties of Somerset and Gloucester (1760). More than half a million enslaved African people were traded by Bristol merchants, many of them destined for the West Indies, where Clementina's uncle made his fortune. *The Miriam and Ira D. Wallach Division of Art, Prints and Photographs: Print Collection, The New York Public Library*

Shortly after Clementina stepped into the chaise, a second note arrived at the school informing the Mills sisters that Clementina would be spending the night at her guardian's house. In reality, she was now in Perry's clutches and, with the treacherous servant acting as chaperone, the party set off on the journey north to Scotland, where girls could marry without parental consent at the age of twelve (boys had to be fourteen). Because there were no legal protections in place, after marriage all of Clementina's property would automatically belong to Perry.

Once the abduction was discovered, Mary Mills, accompanied by her brother, went in pursuit but when she caught up with Perry and Clementina near Carlisle it was too late — they were already married and on their way south. Mary Mills asked Perry if she could speak to 'Miss Clarke', but Perry, a pistol in his hand according to newspaper reports, scoffed and said there was no such person. He had only *Mrs Perry* and the servant in the carriage, and he knew of no business Miss Mills had with either. *The Caledonian Mercury* reported on 31 March that, 'Mrs. Perry has contradicted, by a public advertisement, the suggestion that she was taken away by force, and requested that no credit may be given to a report "injurious to the honour of her husband, and to her own happiness!".'[14]

London fizzed with the story, every episode of which was reported in the newspapers. Scurrilous prints were exhibited publicly. An etching in the British Museum collection shows four horses driven rapidly by two postillions pulling a coach in which a man embraces a young girl, who holds a pistol in her right hand while she flings her doll out of the window. They are followed by a man on a galloping horse who wears an apothecary's mortar and flourishes a pestle in place of a whip. The title is 'Elopement from Bristol — or too many for the Bristol bumbrusher'.[15]

The Times published a paragraph replete with *double entendres* about Mary Mills' encounter with Perry and the pistol:

> A PISTOL in the hands of CLEMENTINA PERRY would be absolutely a very dreadful weapon — were the same PISTOL at all like the lady in its readiness to go off![16]

The couple fled to Europe, a dogged Mary Mills and her brother still on their tail, and it was only when Clementina's friends and family offered an olive branch of forgiveness that they returned to England.

FIG.4 A Visit to the Boarding School by William Ward, after George Morland (date unknown). Educating girls at small boarding-schools was popular with aspirational middle-class families.
Yale Center for British Art, Paul Mellon Collection, B1977.14.12018

Clementina's mother Isobel accepted the fact of the marriage and, fearful that a Gretna Green union was not sufficiently legitimate, insisted that the couple go through another ceremony in London. They were married at St. Leonard's, Shoreditch on 15 October 1792, with Isobel and three other witnesses in attendance. Mary Mills, however, took matters up a level and prosecuted Perry for feloniously stealing Clementina and marrying her against her consent, a capital charge.

When the case came finally before the Bristol court in 1794 Perry was defended by Thomas Erskine, the leading barrister of the day, who had himself eloped to Gretna Green over twenty years previously (and much to his first family's disappointment did so again in 1818). Erskine went head-to-head with William Fielding, the son of the novelist and Justice of the Peace Henry Fielding, who was acting for Mary Mills. It was a tetchy and noisy hearing frequently interrupted by the thousand-strong crowd outside the courthouse shouting 'Perry for ever!'. Clementina, now aged seventeen and pregnant with her second child, took the stand and stated that she knew exactly what she was doing when she got into the liveried chaise. Was this true? Probably not. It is more likely that she wanted to avoid the ignominy of her husband being hanged and her children rendered bastards. No one was surprised when the prosecution failed. Perry was chaired by the jubilant mob, who carried him and Clementina through the streets of Bristol and pulled their carriage.

Perry later took the name of Clementina's benefactor, becoming Richard Vining Perry Ogilvie. He and Clementina produced three children: Richard Perry in 1791, Isabella Carolina Clarke Ogilvie in 1793, and Sarah Christiana Keely Vining Perry in 1798. From the scant information we have we can surmise that their married life was characterised by instability. In 1797 Perry stood unsuccessfully for the parliamentary seat of New Windsor in Berkshire. After a spell in Edinburgh he reinvented himself as a poet, producing several pamphlets of works, including *Fame, Let Thy Glorious Trumpet Sound!*, a eulogy on the victory and death of Lord Nelson, and *The Battle's Hot Hour*. It is likely that Ogilvie squandered at least some of his new-found fortune. In 1810 he was imprisoned in the Abbey (an apartment within Holyrood Palace in Edinburgh) for a debt to his draper. He was also the likely driving force behind a case he and Clementina pursued against her brother.

Perry then headed for St. Mary, Jamaica and the Langley estate in the

FIG.5. Irish Fortune Hunters storming the Bristol Boarding School; or, Potatoe Artillery for ever (1785). Young women were deemed to have a particular interest in military men, and Irish men were seen as the biggest chancers in the game of snagging an heiress. *Yale Center for British Art, Paul Mellon Collection, B1981.25.1649*

parish of St. Thomas in the Vale. He appears to have stayed in Jamaica between 1817 and 1820, possibly longer. In 1817, he was recorded as the owner of 147 enslaved people.[17]

An interesting postscript shows that Clementina was remembered years after the Bristol court case. In 1810 *The Glasgow Herald* reported that 'a female imposter, who passes by the name of Clementina Perry, has been lately laying the inhabitants of Bath, and the neighbouring towns, under contribution. She is a middle-aged woman, of the middle size; she sometimes pretends she came from the island of Jamaica in search of her husband, and is accompanied by a little girl, of about nine years of age, who, it is pretended, can speak nothing but Spanish, having been educated in the island of Cuba.'[18]

Clementina died in Bath in 1813, aged thirty-eight and reputedly in a condition of great poverty.[19]

FIG.6 An idealised view of Llanrumny Estate, St. Mary's, Jamaica, by James Hakewill (between 1820 and 1821). When Clementina Clarke inherited sugar estates unprotected by trusts, she immediately became a target for Richard Vining Perry's financial aspirations.
Yale Center for British Art, Paul Mellon Collection, B1977.14.1960

TWO

HOAX!

THE MYSTERY OF THE STOCKWELL ELOPEMENT

> Let a carriage be procured, and waiting in Park-road with the horses' heads turned to the high road; the ladder of six feet will enable me to get upon the wall at the bottom of the garden, and then in the morning happy shall be the one which, I have no doubt, I shall have to bless as long as I live.
>
> *Letter to 'Mr. Seymour' from 'Maria', The Englishman, 3 January 1830*

THIS STRANGE AND obscure episode involving a magistrate with enemies, two naïve and as yet unidentified men and an equally mysterious and probably fictitious woman, took place in late 1829 and early 1830 close to my home in Stockwell, south London, and came to my attention when I was trawling newspapers for historical stories of local interest.

At the time this drama took place, the Clapham Road, which stretched from the Kennington turnpike (until 1799 a place of execution) to Clapham High Street, was lined with the grand houses of City merchants. After dark, travellers were wise to be wary of robbers. I have tentatively pinpointed the house at the centre of the intrigue as 171 Clapham Road,[20] a now-decaying eighteenth-century mansion standing on the corner with Stockwell Park Road, which for many years

FIG. 7 The Elopement by Thomas Rowlandson (1792). Tales of naïve young boarding-school girls absconding with eager, and impoverished, military men offered plenty of scope for prurient speculation.
Yale Center for British Art, Paul Mellon Collection. B1977.14.346

has been used as a storehouse for a motor accessory shop and is one of the most stunning, and neglected, Georgian buildings in the area. The space in front of the house, where once a garden may have flourished, is a desolate car park, and a tall wall runs along the Stockwell Park Road side. Greenwood's map of 1828 shows a detached building in this position, set back further from the road than the buildings adjacent to it, and an extensive garden behind, matching descriptions of the house.

The facts, such as they are, are clear.[21] In the early evening of Monday 28 December 1829, Charles Leppard, a watchman, spotted two young men wrapped in cloaks and described as 'tall and rather fine-looking' enter an alley by the side of the garden. They were acting suspiciously, signalling to each other using whistles, and generally skulking about. At about 6.30pm Robert Hedger,[22] a magistrate who was the owner of the house, arrived home from Kingston upon Thames, where he had been sitting on the grand jury at the Surrey assizes. Leppard stopped him at the gate and told him about the men, after which they both went in pursuit, the suspects having by then left the site and taken different ways down Clapham Road. Both Leppard and Hedger succeeded in arresting their quarry.

The accoutrements and implements in the possession of the two young men certainly pointed to nefarious intent: a scaling ladder, a loaded gun, watches and thirty-seven gold sovereigns. One of the men was wearing a sailor's blue jacket and trousers under what the newspaper reporter showily referred to as his *rocquelaure* which is, to you and me, a knee-length cloak. The image that comes to mind would not be out of place in a nineteenth-century stage melodrama. Intriguingly, letters from a woman called Maria Wallace addressed to a Mr. Seymour were also discovered on his person.

The young men were duly taken off to the lock-up a mile away at Clapham and the next day put before Thomas Puckle, the local magistrate, where they refused to explain what they had been doing at Hedger's house. They also declined to give their real names, declaring that they would be known only by the pseudonyms George Frederick Seymour and Thomas Junk. They had been led to believe, they claimed, that a young woman at the house needed their assistance and, specifically, wanted to elope with Seymour.

Two days later, Seymour and Junk made another appearance in court, this time at Union Hall, Southwark in front of magistrate

FIG.8 The elopement, a scene from *Stanley Thorn* by Henry Cockton. Thorn, gesturing towards his servant Bob, who is dressed in a lady's cloak and bonnet, attempts to raise Amelia. From *Bentley's Miscellany*, Vol. V (US edition), Jan.–Jun. 1840.
Courtesy of Boston Public Library

Maurice Swabey, where they were represented by the solicitor James Harmer, who was well known for his investigations into miscarriages of justice and often acted for radical politicians. William Hone, a campaigning journalist, writer and playwright, and perpetual thorn in the side of authority, was also in court, his interest probably excited by the identity of the purported victim and prosecutor in the case, Robert Hedger. Hone may have been disappointed that the explanation Harmer offered for his clients' unusual behaviour was not in the least political. It was all in the name of love, or *amour* as the newspapers archly phrased it. Through a third party, Seymour had received several letters claiming to be from a young woman incarcerated in Hedger's house with her mother, who was alleged to be Hedger's sister.

Things became more puzzling when Hedger told the court that a couple of days before the incident, he had himself received an anonymous letter that warned him to expect an attack on his house by robbers, one of whom would be dressed as a sailor. He was due to attend the assizes that day so before he left the house he asked his brother-in-law to remain inside and gave him a brace of guns for protection. The brother-in-law later stated in court that he would have used his weapons if either of the two young men had attempted to scale the garden wall.

A silversmith called Mr. Robins gave a character reference for Seymour and Junk, saying they were 'highly respectable'. As for the young men themselves, they strenuously denied intending to break and enter, a felony for which punishment would be severe. They protested that they had gone through the usual rituals of elopement, hiring a coach for their flight and, in Seymour's case, inquiring about dressmakers able to make suitable clothes for his wife-to-be, who would have to leave most of her wardrobe behind in the escape.

Although they were happy to give their real names in private, they told Maurice Swabey, they refused to divulge their real names in open court in front of journalists. Mr. Swabey found this unacceptable so he remanded them to Horsemonger Lane gaol.

The hearing resumed in the morning, with more details of the plot. William Catchpole,[23] a watchmaker of Fenchurch Street, swore that letters from Seymour to his new fiancée had been left with him and collected by a lady accompanied by a boy and that he knew nothing about the letter sent to Hedger warning of an attack. The coachman hired to carry away the happy couple also gave evidence, saying that he was convinced the two men had gone to Stockwell for the purpose they had described.

The content of one of the letters found on Seymour was read out to the court:[24]

> Dear Sir, — Your letter reached me on Thursday, a few minutes before I got into the carriage on our way to Blackheath, where we have been staying until last night; the engagement of a week's standing was kept a secret from me; you will therefore judge there is no great cordiality existing in our household. Your sentiments are just what I should have expected from the idol of my heart; the world may ridicule the notion of falling in love with an unseen and unknown person, but I have read to little advantage if such cases are not common, and my heart is very treacherous to me indeed if my feelings towards you ever change. I wish you would speedily devise some means for my escape, as I am determined not to remain much longer under my aunt's roof. Our house is situated a small distance from Clapham; it is large, standing detached, and inclose; my bedroom faces the road, and is about 40 feet from the ground. A ladder, which could easily be placed under my window, would enable me to escape, and a post-chaise at hand to convey me to some place of safety, which I should not fear entering under the solemn pledge of your unimpeachable honour and integrity, until a license could be procured for uniting us. Let me have your plans; a light in my bed-room shall indicate I am ready, as well as point out to you the house, and also my person, which, I flatter myself, you will find far from disagreeable. One more letter from you, fully explanatory, shall be the last I will require, and you shall then see I have resolution to put in force your suggestions. I am disturbed — my messenger is faithful — doubt not my love and resolution. In haste, adieu. To-morrow morning my trusty servant makes her weekly appearance. Be courageous and discern, as you shall find me.
>
> Your's [sic] affectionately,
>
> Maria ——

It was obvious to Swabey, and to everyone else in court, that the whole thing was a set-up and that Maria was a figment. He ordered the two men to be released, and did not force them to reveal their identities.

Let's leave the story there for now and turn to the idea that two people who have never met might eagerly agree to bind themselves irrevocably in marriage to each other. Why would they do that? In other words, why did Seymour fall for the hoax? We know nothing of his circumstances, but that he was in need of money or was easily persuaded that his fortune could be made without a great deal of effort seems a reasonable assumption.

Was marriage an extreme measure to take? Not necessarily. As we have seen with the union of Clementina Clarke and Richard Vining Perry in the previous chapter, once Seymour was married, he would have possession of his wife's property, which the author of the letters had described as 'considerable'; after that he could abandon her without much trouble.

Why would Maria, or someone like her, offer marriage in exchange for 'rescue' and the possibility of landing in a worse situation? That is not so easily answered. We could reason that if Hedger was making her life unbearable or dangerous, escaping into marriage, even with a stranger, might be a risk worth taking.

Was the hoaxer trying to harm Hedger or Seymour and Junk or both parties? That is unanswerable as the identities of the young men were never revealed and the perpetrator of the hoax remains a mystery. Robert Hedger, on the other hand, is fairly well documented. He had a fearsome reputation as a Surrey county magistrate and chairman of the Horsemonger Lane sessions. Did that mean that he had enemies? I looked through the newspapers (admittedly a patchy source) for some examples of his decisions, and found one that could indicate an inclination to cruelty. Just over a year before the hoax, Hedger had wanted to sentence a starving and unemployed man whose wife was terminally ill and who had been found guilty of stealing a vice and a brass tap to seven years transportation, and only rowed this back to six months imprisonment when the prisoner made loud and dramatic appeals in court ('For God's sake, think of my wife, who is on her death-bed!').[25]

The controversial New York religious periodical *The Comet* gave an opinion on Hedger in relation to the prosecution of Robert Taylor, a clergyman-turned-freethinker who set up the Christian Evidence Society and attacked the Anglican liturgy. Blasphemy was at the time a criminal offence.

> Robert Hedger was the Chairman of the Court of Sessions, – a man whom no man calls friend or companion; a man who has emanated from one of the vilest hot-beds of vice that London ever contained, and who retains the character and the habits that were there generated. Such was the magistrate who sentenced the virtuous and talented Robert Taylor to two years' imprisonment, and to felons' treatment.[26]

On 29 November 1834 the Radical Richard Carlile, who campaigned for the establishment of universal suffrage and freedom of the press, wrote this of Hedger in *The Scourge*:

> The indictment charges me with having committed a nuisance by the exhibition of effigies in Fleet Street. The foreman of the Grand Jury, which has returned this a true bill, is that selfsame notorious Robert Hedger, who is Chairman of the Surrey Sessions, who was born in a nuisance, brought up in a nuisance, and who has turned out a nuisance to society as a profligate drunkard. His father begat him, and made the fortune he inherits in a common brothel and highwayman's house, that was called the Dog and Duck, in St. George's Fields [Hedger's father was a licensed victualler]. If the man's character were now good, I would not reproach him for the scene of his birth; but it is notoriously bad and hypocritical.[27]

Hedger was certainly not short of critics. Perhaps one or a band of them dreamed up an elaborate way to take revenge on him and the hapless Seymour and Junk at the same time.

THREE

LORD THURLOW'S GRIEF

CAROLINE HERVEY & SAMUEL BROWN

> It is said, that one of the Miss Thurlow's [sic] eloped, from her father's house, on Wednesday morning, for Gretna Green, with a military gentleman. *Hampshire Chronicle, 13 February 1792*

THE POLITICAL CAREER of Edward Thurlow, 1st Baron Thurlow, Lord Chancellor, lasted thirty years but came to an abrupt end on 26 April 1792 after his eldest and favourite daughter, Caroline, a gifted singer, eloped with Samuel Brown, an event that led to a serious breakdown in his mental health.

Lord Thurlow, the son of the Reverend Thomas Thurlow, never married. With Polly Hervey,[28] the daughter of the Dean of Canterbury, he had four 'natural' children: a son Charles, who died as a young man, and three daughters. Two had married: Mary to Sir David Cunyngham and Catharine to the 17th Lord Saltoun.

The devotion of Thurlow to his eldest daughter, twenty-year-old Caroline, was described by her music teacher, Richard Stevens:

> The anxiety of Lord Thurlow that his daughter Caroline should arrive at a great perfection in Music, and in Singing, is beyond my power to describe; tho' a few leading features which I can

FIG.9 Caroline Thurlow's younger sisters, Maria and Catherine, by George Romney (1783). All three girls were the illegitimate and much adored daughters of Edward Thurlow, 1st Baron Thurlow.
Yale University Art Gallery

> mention may give some idea of it. As my time was by no means fully occupied when I first went to Knight's Hill [in Dulwich, south London], I have sat teaching Miss Thurlow sometimes for three hours together; the Chancellor all the while attending, and occasionally giving examples to his daughter of the expression which the words required. I have heard him recite at different times, walking about the Room, and with action, Milton's Morning Hymn; Il Penseroso; Dryden's Ode on St Cecilia's Day; Fletcher's Hence, all ye vain delights, and detached parts of Shakespeare's plays. All the Italian Songs that Miss Thurlow learned to sing, of what sort soever, they were all translated by the Chancellor, in order that his daughter might not be ignorant of the sense, or the expression necessary to their just exhibition.[29]

Caroline eloped with Samuel Brown, who was then a clerk at the Customs House but had previously had a military career, serving with the Yorkshire Light Infantry and rising to the rank of Lieutenant-Colonel and assistant to the Duke of York.

When Lord Thurlow's friend Mr. Hey, at whose house at Coxheath in Kent Caroline was staying, became aware of her relationship with Brown he warned Lord Thurlow, who tried to persuade his daughter to break it off. However, Brown appeared to play the sympathy card with Caroline, growing his beard and neglecting himself until she agreed to take a walk with him. When they were some distance from Hey's house, they climbed into a chaise and four, which was conveniently waiting nearby, and went off to London, shortly afterwards heading for Scotland. The event was immediately hot news. Stevens, the music teacher, learnt of it from Thurlow's coachman while he was at the Lambeth turnpike. The coachman called out, 'He has got her, Sir! He has got her!', dismounted and huddled in a corner to give him the juicy gossip.

Did Caroline have prior knowledge of the plan? Undoubtedly. Before she left, she gave the coachman a letter for her mother, who lived in Dulwich, and another for her father, who was that day sitting in the House of Lords. He was handed the note in the Chamber and was seen to become 'dreadfully agitated and depressed' but could not excuse himself from the debate as there was not enough notice to get a substitute. His peers were 'astonished to see the tears trickle down [his] face, all the time that he sat on the Woolsack; and, wondered what could be the cause!'

At first Thurlow clung to the idea that Caroline had been pressurised into the elopement. He sent an attorney to ask her about the circumstances of her flight. When it clear that Caroline had eloped of her own free will, Thurlow removed Caroline's musical instruments from the family home. He also declared that he would not speak to anyone who remained in communication with her. Catharine agreed to this but Mary declared that 'she never would give up the society of her dear Caroline, but with her life!' Her outburst, which left both Mary and Lord Thurlow in tears, persuaded him to relent but he persisted in rejecting Caroline herself.

At the same time, Lord Thurlow's political career imploded. A committed and ardent Tory and royalist (he is remembered for his epithet 'When I forget my sovereign, may my God forget me'), he finally fell out with William Pitt the Younger and shortly after Caroline's elopement was retired from office. The turning-point was his rudeness to the Whig Lord Grenville, a cousin to Pitt, whose elevation to the peerage he resented. George III created him a baron.

Ten years after the estrangement from her father, Caroline's friend Lord Cadogan wrote to Thurlow to tell him that she was 'alarmingly ill'. Thurlow, who was unwell himself, replied saying, 'Pity and compassion for a loved and favoured daughter, is all I have ever felt, or can ever feel upon her account; but Indignation and Contempt, in a supreme degree, I must ever feel, for the Gang that seduced her from me.' If it meant that she might recover, he would be prepared to see her, although the effort might kill him.

Caroline asked Richard Stevens for advice – he recommended emphatically that she see her father. As he said in his diary, he had observed their relationship at close hand for fifteen years, and 'I never saw anything like his attachment to her from any parent'.

Stevens witnessed the reunion. When Caroline's carriage drew up at the door of her parents' home in Dulwich, she was in such a state of prostration that she had to be carried to the parlour. She was given a dose of hartshorn (ammonium bicarbonate) to revive her. In tears, she said: 'My dear, dear, Father, I have suffered ten years of the most dreadful misery, in losing your dear society and affection. I know my error, I know what I have lost, don't reproach me! but pray, pity and forgive me?' Thurlow was unable to speak and sat grasping her hand, staring at the floor.

'There was a time, my dear Father, when I should not have experienced this dreadful silence. Oh! think how terrible it must be to me now?' she said.

'Oh name it not! Name it not my child! for God Almighty's sake! name it not, if you mean to save my life!' he replied.

According to Stevens, 'the Agony, and horrible exertion, with this these words were uttered, made his Lordship so exceedingly ill, that he was obliged to leave the room. Hartshorn spirit, Brandy, and a variety of restoratives were brought by Bissy [the valet], and Mrs. Harvey, in order to relieve him from fainting and the violence of his uncommon agitation.'

Father and daughter built on their reconciliation, with many visits ensuing. Lord Thurlow died at Brighton on 12 September 1806. Samuel Brown died in 1855 and Caroline three years later, aged eighty-six. They had had a large number of children, possibly as many as ten.

FOUR

'A MAN OF FASHION'

ANN WADE & CHARLES BASELEY

> Mr. Charles Baseley... represented himself as an acquaintance of Lord Yarmouth. He drove a tilbury with two horses, was attended by two grooms, and is supposed to be in embarrassed circumstances, as on leaving Weymouth, he obtained £50 of his landlord.
>
> *Bury and Norwich Post, 2 November 1814*

ANN WADE, THE only child and heiress of Albany Wade and his wife Jane Wooler, was orphaned in 1806, when she was nine. Albany, aged only thirty-two, died in March, apparently of consumption, and his wife followed a few months later, of the same cause. Ann was lined up to take possession of her father's fortune when she turned twenty-one, including real estate, mines and collieries in the north east of England. She was also entitled to an annual income of £5,000. Until then her property was protected by the Court of Chancery.

That did not mean she was not vulnerable to predators. In 1814, aged seventeen, Ann, who was 'rather handsome',[30] was living in the care of her guardian Mr. Broughton, of Reigate, Surrey, in the fashionable seaside resort of Weymouth on the Dorset coast, where Charles Henry Baseley, the impecunious son of a clergyman of dubious reputation, who fancied himself 'a man of fashion', groomed her using her governess and domestic servants, and his own sister.

Ann and Charles absconded on the night of 11 October, after which Broughton went in pursuit. An advertisement appeared in papers across the country, in which a reward of two hundred guineas (£210) was offered and the runaways were described in detail. Ann Wade was:

> five feet six inches high, black hair, fair brown complexion, with regular striking features, is near-sighted, and wears an eye-glass with a gold chain; was dressed when taken away in a morning bathing-dress of nankeen, a coarse straw bonnet, with green veil, apple green scarf shawl, and French green and yellow silk neck handkerchief. The said Charles H. Baseley is 24 years of age, light hair, and fresh complexion, with thin sandy whiskers, about 6 feet high; wore a blue coat with buff waistcoat.[31]

Her friends were said to be 'inconsolable' and Ann was urged to contact them. Clergymen and parish clerks were warned not to publish their banns or to marry them.

In London Broughton tracked down the couple, who had issued banns at St. Saviour's, Southwark, and managed to prevent them marrying.[32] Ann returned home but this failure did not stop Baseley from trying again. He contrived this time to embed his agents in Broughton's household. Mary Julia Marie, who took a job as Ann's governess, was in Baseley pay, and her husband Simon Marie offered Mrs. Broughton £10,000 if she would hand Ann over. The sums involved were eye-watering but also fantastical. Baseley, who had had to borrow £50 for his first attempt to run away with Ann, was without means.

In April 1815 the couple were on the run again. Banns were recorded in the parish register of the Church of St. Marylebone in Westminster, where another parish clerk later scored through the entry and added a note: 'Forbidden by an injunction from the Court of Chancery'.[33]

In the end, however, the efforts of Ann's friends were in vain. Baseley again ran off with Ann, this time from her guardian's house in Brighton, and on 27 May 1815 they tied the knot in Gretna Green, followed a few months later by a ceremony in the Established church in Edinburgh. Ann was mimicking a pattern set by her own parents, who had eloped in 1793 and also married at Gretna Green.

FIG.10 Weymouth by J.M.W. Turner (c. 1811), where Ann Wade became a target of fortune-hunter Charles Baseley.
Yale Center for British Art, Paul Mellon Collection, B1977.14.6297

Charles's father Thomas, the disreputable clergyman, may have assisted the couple in their successful flight to Scotland. Charles's three times great-grandson Christopher Beavis has supplied me with the text of this note left by his great-grandfather, R.F.C. Tear:

> In the case of Mr. Baseley's father's complicity in the elopement, an affidavit was put in on his own and his wife's behalf pleading that they had no hand in the affair, nor had they made any suggestions or taken any action in that direction. It was however hinted by the other side that the Rev. Baseley was not above reproach, he having been mixed up in a notorious scandal.
>
> This low opinion of Baseley Snr was based on a statement by a Mr. Leach at a hearing of the Court of Chancery, 6 December 1815... As counsel for the paternal uncle (Thomas Wade, Ann's nearest relative), he sought to denigrate the defendant's father with the comment, 'His father was a clergyman, but not of very high reputation, his character having been tainted by some circumstance of public notoriety; and so far from being in affluent circumstances, he was now living as a dealer in pictures.'

Ann and Charles lived in Scotland while petitions on their behalf were submitted to Lord Eldon, the Lord Chancellor, who refused them all. Ann's uncle Thomas Wade prosecuted Baseley, his sister Sophia and their servants; Baseley was ordered to appear in court. He held out until December, when he was promptly committed to the Fleet prison, remaining there until his wife turned twenty-one in 1818.

In March 1816 Ann applied to the Court of Chancery for £500 to cover the expenses of the birth of her first child and the Lord Chancellor took this opportunity to settle her entire fortune so that Baseley could not touch it. Ann gave birth to Charles Albany Baseley at her home in Dover Street, London, on 6 April 1816. Emily Ann and Thomas were born in the Fleet prison on 3 April 1817 and 4 May 1818. Ann and Charles went on to have eight further children. In April 1821 the King granted Baseley's request to use Ann's surname and coat of arms. It was a minor victory. The bigger one was that he was that although none of the Wade estate came formally into his possession, through Ann he was able to make use of it during her lifetime.

The 1841 census showed Ann and Charles Wade living in Erith, Kent with five children. Charles was described as 'independent'. Ten years later, they lived at 7 Douglas Place, Walnut Tree Road in east Greenwich with two daughters, a son and a granddaughter; Charles was a 'landed proprietor'. They were still at Douglas Place in 1861, now with a son, two daughters and two granddaughters. After Ann died in 1863, Charles promptly married Cecilia Swayne, his grandchildren's Irish nursery governess, who was forty-three years his junior. Their son Henry was born in 1866. In the 1871 census, when the family lived at 153 Charles Street, Tower Hamlets, Charles described himself as a landowner.

Here again, Christopher Beavis is able to add some detail: 'I have a bundle of letters from the time of Charles's second marriage from the solicitor handling the estate and between the surviving grown-up children of the marriage after Ann's death.' In one of them the solicitor writes of Charles:

> The lost sheep has returned to the fold or at least your father has paid me a visit and seemed very humiliated at the position in which his conduct has placed him. He made the best case he could — stated that it was never his intention to desert you, that he had been very ill and laid up with a pain in his foot which had disabled him from getting about of which he bore strong evidence by wearing an easy shoe — and moreover had never been out of London but had been obliged to keep secret on account of the Law Proceedings going on against him. This was all very well but I asked if it prevented him from writing, to which he gave no answer.

In another letter, from Charles Harrison of Bedford Row dated 3 March 1866, the solicitor wrote:

> Your father is apathetic & seems totally indifferent to doing anything except getting money out of my hands.

Charles Henry Wade died in 1874, aged about eighty-three. Henry, the son he had with Cecilia, died in 1881, aged fifteen. Cecilia can be found in the censuses as an inmate at Islington Workhouse in north London where she remained until at least 1911, when she was seventy-four, and died in Lewisham, southeast London, four years later.

FIVE

A TRAGICAL DRAMA

AUGUSTA FOSTER NICHOLSON & JOHN GILES

> Miss N[icholson] had a bed room to herself, and got up every morning before five o'clock, and conversed with her lover out of the window. The correspondence continued about five weeks previous to the elopement. *Oxford Journal, 11 November 1809*

IN THE AUTUMN of 1809, accompanied by her stepmother, Augusta Foster Nicholson, the nineteen-year-old daughter of Colonel James Nicholson, arrived in the fashionable town of Tunbridge Wells in Kent, expecting to enjoy the famous spa, fine assembly rooms and lively theatres and, quite possibly, hoping to find a suitable husband.

Augusta was certainly a catch, as she had what can only be described as huge expectations. Through the unfortunate but timely deaths of eight relatives over the course of six years, she was due, on her twenty-first birthday, to come into a fortune of £14,000. We have no way of knowing whether John Giles, a 'comedian' — today we might call him a comedy actor or a variety performer — knew that she was in line for this windfall when one day in October, according to later newspaper reports, he offered to carry her library books. Incidentally, we can speculate that the library in question was Sprange's Circulating Library on

FIG.11 Tunbridge Wells from Frant Forest by Joseph Josiah Dodd (c. 1826), aft. Robert Havell. The town was noted for its supposedly health-giving spa. *Yale Center for British Art, Paul Mellon Collection. B1978.43.866*

The Pantiles, close to the theatre where John was a member of Mrs. Baker's Company.[34]

If the newspapers are to be believed, the next evening, Augusta and her stepmother went to the theatre and sat in the box closest to the stage. Augusta came prepared: unnoticed by her stepmother, she dropped a note to John in which she declared her love and encouraged him to pay his addresses. Meetings between the lovers followed. Someone must have noticed and told Mrs. Nicholson, who tried to put an end to it by confining Augusta to the house, but Augusta was one step ahead and continued the romance by passing *billets-doux* to John through the keyhole of the street door and talking to him at the window in the morning, before the rest of the household was up. This went on for five weeks until Augusta and John made a decision: they would elope to London and get married.

John was 'destitute of the most needful article, money, for carrying on such an exploit,'[35] so he persuaded his friend, a Mr. Smith, a fellow performer with Mrs. Baker, to lend him some £30, which was all the poor fellow had. To keep their plans secret, he and Smith walked to Sevenoaks, a distance of about twelve miles, where they hired a chaise and four and drove it back to Tunbridge to collect Augusta. Smith stayed outside the town while John dashed into Tunbridge to collect his sweetheart. She took with her only one change of clothes.

Mrs. Nicholson promptly employed the renowned Bow Street runner Harry Adkins and his brother to track down the runaway lovers. They quickly picked up the scent and discovered that Augusta and John had reached the White Hart Inn at Bromley on the outskirts of London, where they had changed horses and proceeded at full gallop to Marshgate Turnpike on Westminster Road where they hopped into a hackney coach. From there they travelled to 47 South Molton Street in the West End, where Augusta lodged for two days. In order to preserve her reputation, John stayed elsewhere.

After Augusta and John fled again, the trail went cold but the officers then received information that they were at 37 Westmorland Place, City Road, lodging with a Mrs. Steele. Adkins knocked on the door and asked for Giles; the landlady replied that he was eating. Adkins entered and addressed John by name. He answered but denied he had ever been to Tunbridge Wells. His protestations came to nothing after Dr. Cardale, solicitor and trustee to the Nicholson family, arrived

FIG.12 The Lending Library, by Isaac Cruikshank (1800–11). The romance between comedy actor John Giles and heiress Augusta Nicholson supposedly began when he offered to carry her borrowed books.
Yale Center for British Art, Paul Mellon Collection. B1975.4.867

and identified Augusta. The lovers rushed into each other's arms and swore their mutual attachment. Augusta agreed to go with the officers only if she could first go upstairs to collect her wedding ring. It seems that the couple were on their uppers. They had been due to marry at St. Marylebone but had already spent the £30 lent by Mr Smith and owed their landlady for board and lodging.[36]

At the Court of Chancery, Smith at first denied his involvement but was told he must produce Augusta on pain of prosecution for conspiracy. John Giles, Mr. Stubbs of South Molton Street and Mrs. Steele of Westmoreland Place received notices to appear before the Lord Chancellor the same day and Giles was briefly imprisoned in the Fleet.

Given the stubborn opposition of Augusta's family, it surprised me to find that the couple married on 22 February 1810. However, they chose to do so at Braddan on the Isle of Man, which was outside the jurisdiction of the English courts. Neither Augusta nor John gave their fathers' names on the register, which might indicate that they had once again eloped. Augusta was pregnant. Tragically, she died soon after giving birth to a son, leaving her husband and child with nothing – she was four days short of her majority and thus never came into her fortune. That money was now her brother's. He was a naval captain and promptly set sail to England to claim it. However, in September 1811 he died en route and, as there were no other legatees, the money reverted to Augusta's son.[37]

SIX

THE SHRIGLEY ABDUCTION

ELLEN TURNER & EDWARD GIBBON WAKEFIELD

MARRIED — On the 8th inst., Edward Gibbon Wakefield, Esq., to Ellen only daughter of W. Turner, esq. of Shrigley Park, in the County of Chester. *Morning Post, 11 March 1826*

FIFTEEN-YEAR-OLD heiress Ellen Turner of Pott Shrigley near Macclesfield in Cheshire was the only child of William Turner, who owned calico printing and spinning mills. In 1826, she was abducted from her Liverpool boarding-school by Edward Gibbon Wakefield. The case became known as the Shrigley Abduction.[38]

Edward Gibbon Wakefield was born on 20 March 1796 in London, the second of nine children of Edward Wakefield and Susanna, *née* Crash, and educated at Westminster School and Edinburgh High School. He trained as a lawyer and entered the diplomatic service in 1814 as secretary to the British envoy at Turin. While in London in June 1816 he eloped with sixteen-year-old Eliza Ann Pattle, a ward of Chancery. Two children were born to the marriage but Eliza died in 1820, shortly after giving birth to the second.

Edward and his brother William Wakefield lived in Paris, where in December 1825 they made the acquaintance of Frances Davies, who was from Macclesfield, in Cheshire, and was visiting the city with her elderly schoolteacher father. Wakefield later confessed that Ellen Turner had come up in conversation as 'a very fine girl, and the heiress to one of the largest fortunes in the county, and that he was determined to possess himself of her'. The Turner estate at Pott Shrigley was less than five miles from the centre of Macclesfield, so perhaps Frances had heard gossip about the Turners and their fortune.

On her return to Macclesfield in early February, Frances called on an acquaintance, Miss Brocklehurst, and pestered her for an introduction to the Turner family. She expressed particular interest in meeting Ellen and was disappointed to learn that she was back at school. At the beginning of March 1826, the Wakefield brothers arrived in Macclesfield, and Frances and her father set about introducing them to local society. They rode around the town and visited Pott Shrigley, where they familiarised themselves with the grounds and the house. They befriended Thomas Grimsditch, Mr. Turner's solicitor, and learned that the two men were planning to travel to London the following Monday. They also discovered that Ellen's mother, Jane Turner, had a neurological illness and suffered from a form of paralysis.

The next day, Edward and William travelled twenty miles to Manchester, hiring en route a Frenchman called Thevenot as manservant. After buying a second-hand carriage for forty pounds, all three set off for Liverpool, reaching the city at two o'clock the next day. Here they composed a letter to Ellen's schoolmistress, Elizabeth Daulby, purporting to come from a doctor and claiming that Mrs. Turner was desperately ill.

On 7 March 1827, Thevenot, pretending to be a servant employed by Ellen's father, called at the school. After some initial misgivings, Elizabeth Daulby released Ellen to him, thinking that she would be taken straight home. Of course, she was not.

First she was transported to Manchester, where she met Edward Wakefield for the first time. '[Wakefield] said he was commissioned by my papa to take me to him... that it was the state of my papa's affairs which had induced him to send for me home,' Ellen said later in court. Wakefield admitted to her that the news of her mother's illness was a lie, and promised they were going to meet up with her father further north at Kendal. There she was told her that her father had not arrived but would meet her in Carlisle, even further north. During the journey the Wakefields claimed that one of the banks her father used had failed

FIG.13 Edward Gibbon Wakefield in 1826 by Benjamin Holl 'from a drawing by A. Wivell in the possession of Danl. Wakefield Esqr.'
Courtesy of National Library of Australia

but that they had arranged a loan of £60,000 from their uncle, who happened to be a banker himself. Then they told her that another of her father's banks had failed, and that their uncle was demanding security for his loan in the shape of the Shrigley estate, and that Mr. Turner's solicitor Mr. Grimsditch had suggested that she marry Edward Wakefield. The effect would be that, 'the property would be mine... It would be in my power to turn my papa out-of-doors, if I liked.'

The story the Wakefields concocted was more plausible than perhaps it seems to us now. The commercial landscape at that time was highly unstable. A friend of Ellen's had had to leave the school the previous year because her father's business had failed and he could no longer afford the fees and Ellen's father had recently joked with her that should his business fail, she would have to do the same.

Ellen's father was not at Carlisle, where, according the Wakefields, he had had to hide in a back room with Grimsditch and was now fleeing for the Scottish border, pursued by sheriff's men.

'[Wakefield] said that my papa requested, if I ever loved him, that I would not hesitate... to accept Mr. Wakefield as a husband,' recalled Ellen in court. Edward Wakefield and Ellen married at Gretna Green and returned to Carlisle, Ellen expecting to fall into her father's arms but he had, said Wakefield, already left for London.

Thevenot now dropped out of the narrative, as did Edward's brother William. Late in the evening of Friday 10 March, three days after Ellen was abducted, she and Wakefield arrived at the Brunswick Hotel in Hanover Square, London, supposedly still trying to catch up with her father. Here an unknown friend of Wakefield's warned him that the game was up and he was a wanted man. Wakefield now told Ellen that her father was in Calais on urgent business and they must follow him there.

The next day the marriage between Edward Wakefield and Ellen Turner was announced in the newspapers. Mr. Grimsditch obtained a warrant from the magistrate at Bow Street and with Ellen's uncles, Robert Turner and Henry Critchley, and the Bow Street runner John Ellis went in pursuit, reaching Calais on the 15th. They found Wakefield in the courtyard of Quillac's hotel and told him that they had a warrant and a despatch from George Canning, the Foreign Secretary, to the British ambassador in Paris. They demanded to see Ellen and eventually she was brought out to them.

'Well, Mr. Grimsditch, I assure you, upon my honour, that Miss Turner is the same Miss Turner as she was when I took her away; there has been no consummation of the marriage,' announced Wakefield. However, he insisted the marriage was legal and 'claimed her as his wife'. 'I am not your wife, I will never go near you again – you have deceived me,' said Ellen. The warrant not being valid in France, Grimsditch went to a local magistrate to force Wakefield to hand Ellen over, but by the time he returned to the hotel, Wakefield had given in.

The trial of the Wakefields and Frances Davies (who was not present in court and had at some point married the Wakefields' father) took place at Lancaster on 23 March 1827. Thevenot had fled.

On the evidence of fraud it was an open and shut case, with a string of pub landladies, grooms and waiters giving evidence that Ellen had arrived in the company of the Wakefields, who had controlled her and prevented them from speaking directly to her. However, the Wakefields' barrister, the celebrated James Scarlett (later Lord Abinger), attempted to show that Ellen was legally married and for that reason should not be allowed to give evidence against her husband. A long discussion took place on whether the marriage could be proved to be legal and whether it took place by force, with Scarlett arguing that no force was used and the prosecution asserting that intimidation and the threat of harm to her family amounted to force. As the *Caledonian Mercury* put it:

> Wakefield's case has its difficulties as well as its peculiarities. Miss Turner, in the first place, is not an heiress, in the strict sense of the term; but that is not the principal difficulty. The gist of the crime of abduction lies in the forcible marriage. Now the young lady was carried away in England, where abduction is a crime, and she was married in Scotland, where such abduction is no crime at all; where the law supposes every woman in a capacity for marriage as soon as she is fourteen years of age [it was actually twelve], and holds all marriages valid if contracted above that age, whether sanctioned by parents or not. If Mr Wakefield be tried for running away with Miss Turner, and marrying her, he cannot be tried in England, for the crime was not completed there; and if he be tried in Scotland, he must be acquitted, because the law of Scotland does not recognise the offence.[39]

The prosecuting barrister was keen to stress that Ellen did not share a room with her new husband, the implication being that no sexual acts occurred. In court, defence barrister James Scarlett tried to push the prosecution into withdrawing by insinuating that Ellen and Wakefield had indeed had sexual contact:

> ...before the marriage she sat on Mr. Wakefield's knee, with an appearance of the greatest fondness... She freely gave her consent [to the marriage in Scotland]... She was hanging upon Mr. Wakefield's arm in the most affectionate manner... they were... a very loving couple... Every body knows the age of sixteen to one girl is very different to the age of sixteen to another girl.

At half-past seven the jury retired and after forty-five minutes returned with verdicts of guilty against all three defendants on the conspiracy charge. The Wakefield brothers were also guilty of abduction and were taken off to Lancaster Castle gaol. On 14 May, Edward and William Wakefield appeared at the Court of King's Bench in Westminster Hall in London, where they were sentenced to three years in prison, Edward in Newgate and William in Lancaster. Despite Wakefield's efforts, the marriage was annulled by Parliament and two years later Ellen, still only seventeen, was legally married to Thomas Legh, a wealthy neighbour. She died in childbirth two years later.

In prison, Wakefield became preoccupied with issues around punishment and rehabilitation. He advocated the development of colonisation and with William became an early leader in the settlement of New Zealand. He was published widely. He died in New Zealand in 1862. His obituary in the *Daily Telegraph* opined that 'administrative and constructive reform' in the British Empire 'can scarcely be traced to the single hand of any other man'. Society had clearly forgiven, and perhaps forgotten, his shameful history of child abduction.

SEVEN

AN IRREGULAR MARRIAGE

ARTHUR ANNESLEY POWELL & JEMIMA NEATE

While working on diaries of Christiana Fanny Chapman (1775–1871), Georgian historian and genealogist SARAH MURDEN came across the story of a young man in possession of a vast fortune and Jemima Neate, an ambitious woman in search of an opportunity

ARTHUR ANNESLEY ROBERTS was born on 15 April 1767, the son of Elizabeth *née* Powell and William Roberts, and was baptised at the church of St. George, Hanover Square, London. In 1774, at the tender age of seven, he was sent to Harrow School to be educated. Ten years later, he went up to Wadham College, Oxford.[40] He was by then a wealthy young man. A few months earlier, his unmarried maternal uncle, John Powell, the owner of Quex House in Birchington, Kent, died, leaving the majority of his estate to Arthur, his eldest nephew, on the condition that he change his surname to Powell.

The estate Arthur inherited included nearly £160,000 of stocks and mortgages as well as extensive land and properties. However, he was legally still an 'infant', being under the age of twenty-one. Although the name change was not ratified until 1789 — it required an act of Parliament, which additionally confirmed that 'the fruit of Powell's body would also be entitled to continue to inherit the estate from him'

FIG.14 The Oxford Macaroni, etching by Mary Darly, published in the album 'Caricatures, Macaronies & Characters by sundry ladies gentlemen artists &c.' (1772). A dandy was a young man who affected foreign manners and style.
Yale Center for British Art, Paul Mellon Collection, B1977.14.11354

— Arthur was known as Powell immediately after his uncle's death.[41]

About three years before his inheritance, while he was a student, Arthur met Jemima Neate, ten years his senior and the daughter of William Neate, a merchant who had suffered huge financial losses as a result of the American War of Independence, and Christiana *née* Appleton. We can guess that Arthur and Jemima first encountered each other on the Isle of Thanet in Kent — among the properties Arthur inherited was Kingsgate Castle, only two miles from St. Peters, where Jemima's mother lived. Whatever the history of their relationship, the facts are clear. On 11 July 1786, Arthur Annesley Powell married 28-year-old Jemima Neate at Coldstream in Scotland.

Arthur's family was not best pleased but for unknown reasons it took eighteen months for his father, acting on Arthur's behalf, to apply to have the marriage annulled.[42] However, as the minimum age for boys to marry in Scotland was fourteen, the union was deemed to be legal.

In his petition, William Roberts used the argument that Arthur was not competent to marry, alleging that Jemima was skilled in 'the arts and management of crafty' and that Arthur was 'a youth of very weak faculties'. He also claimed that Jemima and her sister and other members of the family exercised 'an undue and improper influence over the great weakness of his [Arthur's] understanding to entrap him into the Celebration of Marriage with Jemima, secretly and clandestinely without the consent of his father'.

According to Arthur's father, at about six o'clock on the morning of 8 July 1786, at their father's house, Jemima and her sister Christiana gave Arthur tea in which they had mixed an unknown substance. When he became drowsy he was bundled into a post-chaise with members of the Neate family and promptly taken off towards Scotland. He was comatose throughout the journey.

At midnight on 10 July, they reached the Bee Hive Inn in Cornhill in County Durham, about a mile and a half from the border with Scotland. The women sent a messenger to procure a parson and subsequently Richard Powley arrived, describing himself as the Episcopal Minister of Kelso in North Britain,[43] and agreed his fees with Christiana (it turned out later that Powley's clerical credentials were dubious). Jemima, Christiana, Richard Powley and Arthur piled into another chaise and proceeded across the Tweed to Coldstream. Arthur put up no resistance.

The marriage between Arthur and Jemima took place at George

Weatherhead's inn at Coldstream at about one o'clock on 11 July, officiated by Richard Powley. The party then swiftly returned to London. Both *The Public Advertiser* and *General Advertiser* of 15 July announced the marriage but provided no details of where or when it took place.

The couple remained together for about three years after which they went their separate ways. There was no judgement in Arthur's father's case and the marriage seems not to have been successfully rescinded. Jemima not only retained the Powell surname throughout her life but received an annual settlement of £500 from her husband which is about £30,000 in 2023 money.

Arthur pursued a career in the military. The next time we hear of him is in 1809 when he shot and killed Charles John Carey, Lord Falkland in a duel over a jocular insult.[44] He died, aged forty-eight on 28 June 1813 at Whewell, Hampshire as a result of a fall from his horse.[45] Arthur's brother John Powell Roberts inherited Quex House and duly changed his name to Powell, becoming John Powell Powell.

Jemima Powell died in 1836, and was buried at Walcot, Bath.

EIGHT

'THESE FEELINGS RIPENED INTO LOVE'

SYDNEY HAMILTON & BENJAMIN BERESFORD

> One [affidavit] in particular stated that Mr. B. ... gave a manifest Proof of what had been his Inducement for coming there; for instead of preaching the Word, and conducting himself like a serious Divine, he employed himself during the whole Ceremony in ogling Miss H. and endeavouring to catch her Attention.
>
> *Derby Mercury, 8 December 1780*

ON THE NIGHT of 1 November 1780, at her mother's home in Pinner, a village north of London, fifteen-year-old Sydney Hamilton went to bed early, pleading a headache. Her bedroom, which she shared with her companion Sarah Dawson and a maid, could be accessed only through her mother's chamber. Whether she changed her clothes and jumped into bed ready to sneak past her sleeping parent, whether she waited until her room-mates were asleep and hid herself in a little-used part of the house, varies in accounts of her extraordinary case. Whatever happened, with her mother's maid Letitia Sutcliffe, she escaped the house and fled to the Queen's Head, a nearby inn, where she joined the 31-year-old Reverend Benjamin Beresford, born a cobbler's son but now chaplain to the Duke of Bedford. They set off for Gretna Green at two in the morning and were married there the next day.

This story, which reads at times like the plot of an overwrought gothic novel, has many troubling aspects, not least of which is the youth of the bride and the substantial age difference between her and her husband. Sydney, shy to the point of timorous, had been sent to boarding-school but was so unhappy she had been brought home, but life there cannot have been much of an improvement. Her mother, who was separated from her father, was hugely ambitious, impossible to please and highly controlling. Mrs. Hamilton (*née* Jane Rowan, the daughter of an Irish lawyer), quite reasonably fearing that the enormous fortune her daughter would come into made her prey to fortune-hunters, decided to keep her closely confined. She was also physically and emotionally cruel to her, on occasion beating her, and making a show of favouring Sydney's companion Sarah Dawson, who was the daughter of a former neighbour in Ireland.

The Reverend Beresford, who was a frequent guest in the house, witnessed Mrs. Hamilton's ill-treatment of her daughter. As he later wrote,

> Mrs. Hamilton seemed to enjoy a malevolent satisfaction in taking occasion to mortify her daughter by a contemptuous mode of opposing her opinions and sentiments; and Miss Hamilton appeared to feel acutely this unkind maternal triumph.

In a self-serving pamphlet, Beresford claimed that at first he felt merely 'pity and concern' for Sydney, but later, 'by a natural progress' this 'ripened into love', until they were, with the help of the maid Letitia Sutcliffe, who was the clandestine wife of his own manservant, meeting in secret. Astonishingly, Mrs. Hamilton, despite watching her child like a hawk, was oblivious and assumed that the object of Beresford's affections was Sarah Dawson (ironically Sarah later married Sydney's brother with Mrs. Hamilton's blessing). According to Beresford, the plan to elope was Sydney's and the two of them did so in full knowledge that they risked her disinheritance, assuming they would be able to live on the funds Sydney held in her own right and the continued generosity of Beresford's wealthy patrons.

When Sydney's absence was discovered, Mrs. Hamilton rushed to London, where her lawyers advised her to petition the Lord Chancellor for an injunction and prepared a deposition in which she rebutted claims that she had mistreated her daughter.

What followed was a shocking and protracted legal battle over the control of Sydney and the legality of the marriage that extended across the Channel to the French royal court. Throughout, it was characterised by extreme malice on the part of Mrs. Hamilton and suspiciously insistent self-justification on the part of Beresford.[46]

The couple learned of the injunction when they returned from Scotland. It cannot have been a surprise as Sydney was below the age of consent in England. In an attempt to regularise the Scottish marriage by marrying again in England, Beresford first hid Sydney at the home of a dressmaker in St. Marylebone in London, and published banns at St. Katharine Cree in Aldgate, an obscure church in the City.[47] After that he took her to live with him in Duke Street in the West End. However, as a consequence of the scandal, Beresford lost his position with the Duke of Bedford and now had no means of support. In desperation, Sydney went to her mother's house in Great Marlborough Street to beg forgiveness. There, in Beresford's words, Mrs. Hamilton managed to 'work a change in her daughter's affections'; on 10 January 1781, when he went to collect her, he was informed that she had left three hours earlier. Mrs. Hamilton refused to tell him where she had been taken and set about suing him and Letitia Sutcliffe in the Court of King's Bench.

Sydney was in Lille in northern France and, now pregnant, confined in a lunatic asylum. Meanwhile, in London Beresford obtained a writ of *habeas corpus* requiring Mrs. Hamilton to produce her. Now Mrs. Hamilton herself fled to Lille and took an apartment, where Sydney joined her. Beresford discovered their location and also went to Lille, where he and two sheriffs burst into the apartment and persuaded Sydney to sign a paper stating that she loved him and wanted to resume married life with him. The Court of Lille attested this, but Mrs. Hamilton appealed to a higher court at Douai.

On 10 August Sydney gave birth to baby Sophia and Mrs. Hamilton had the child registered at the local church as the 'product of a disputed marriage', indicating that her legitimacy was uncertain. At this point the case moved into the sphere of the French royal court, where Mrs. Hamilton, with the assistance of two known reprobates (according to Beresford), Dr. Keary, an Irish surgeon, and Monsieur de Limon, a disgraced lawyer, appealed to Louis XVI for a *lettre de cachet* (an order signed by the French king). She also managed to gain a power of attorney from her estranged husband, who had superior rights over his daughter, so that she could act of his behalf.

On his return to France after a short visit to England, Beresford was dragged from his bed, flung into the prison of the Grand Châtelet in Paris and charged with abduction and *mésalliance* (marrying while unsuitable), a crime that did not exist in English law. However, he managed to gain the attention of the Parlement of Paris, which saw his case as a test of their strained relationship with Versailles. In a display of independence, they gave judgement against Mrs. Hamilton and had Beresford released. Mrs. Hamilton was ordered to pay costs and £50,000 in damages, to be held in trust for Sophia. All parties were ordered to return to England and settle in the English courts.

Mrs. Hamilton, enraged and vengeful, refused to leave and set about pulling strings. With the help of Keary and de Limon she had the Parlement's decision reversed by royal decree. After this, judging that it would be best to allow the dust to settle, she remained in Paris and placed Sydney in a convent near Versailles.[48]

Beresford returned to London with Sophia and published a pamphlet in which he detailed his mother-in-law's behaviour. He alleged that in Lille her plan had been to conceal the baby's birth, foster it with a local woman, place it in the poorhouse and marry Sydney off to 'some man of fashion'.[49]

A reconciliation between Sydney and Beresford must have taken place at a later date – the marriage produced at least two further children: Harriett in 1789 when Sydney was twenty-four and Hamilton Sidney in 1792. Mrs. Hamilton died in Ireland in 1793 at the age of sixty-four. Benjamin died in 1819 and Sydney in 1827.

Throughout this woeful tale, one voice is notably absent, that of poor Sydney, dragged from pillar to post, deprived of her child and badgered by one side or the other.

NINE

THE LADIES OF LLANGOLLEN

ELEANOR BUTLER & SARAH PONSONBY

The two ladies... found means to elope together; but, being soon overtaken, they were each brought back by their respective relations. Many attempts were renewed to draw Miss Butler into marriage; but, upon her solemnly and repeatedly declaring that nothing could induce her to wed any one, her parents ceased to persecute her by any more offers. *Hereford Journal, 28 July 1790*

ON THE NIGHT of 30 March 1778, at Woodstock House in County Kilkenny, Ireland, 23-year-old Sarah Ponsonby, wearing men's clothing, armed with a pistol and holding her little dog Frisk, climbed out of her bedroom window. She was on her way to meet her 'beloved', Lady Eleanor Butler, thirty-nine, who was also disguised as a man. Together they intended to catch a boat for Wales and start a new life away from their families.[50]

Why did they feel compel to abscond? Sarah lived with her guardians Sir William Fownes and his wife Betty, whose health was deteriorating. To Sarah's alarm, Sir William had begun targeting her as his second wife. She had grown close to Eleanor, who had been drafted in ten years earlier as her minder and teacher while she attended a school close to Kilkenny Castle.

Eleanor, the youngest daughter of the Earl of Ormonde of Kilkenny Castle, was bookish and sharp-witted and, as she was resolutely unmarried, her aristocratic, Irish Catholic family had plans to send her to a convent in France.

It was an unbearable situation. Facing permanent separation, the women formulated a plan to flee. Travelling on horseback, they rode overnight to Waterford, only to find that their ship was not sailing, and took refuge in a barn. Here they were discovered and hauled back to their respective homes. At this point Sarah became ill with a fever, and Eleanor ran away again – and hid in Sarah's bedroom. At this point, the families gave up. The Ormondes refused to have Eleanor back and Sarah's family gave her permission to leave.

Two months later, along with Sarah's faithful maid Mary Carryl, they settled in Llangollen in Denbighshire, Wales. In 1780 they moved to a five-roomed cottage they renamed Plas Newydd (New Place) and which they went into considerable debt to improve, developing it in the Gothic style with Welsh oak panelling, pointed arches, stained glass windows and an extensive library.

Although they were mocked, mostly for their style – top hats, plain black riding habits and powdered hair – and there was plenty of speculation about the nature of their friendship, they had genuine admirers. Among the famous visitors they received at Plas Newydd were Sir Walter Scott, Josiah Wedgwood and William Wordsworth, who dedicated a sonnet to them:

Sisters in love, a love allowed to climb
Ev'n on this earth, above the reach of time

They were also an inspiration to the now famous lesbian diarist Anne Lister, 'Gentleman Jack', who visited them in 1822 and was so excited at the prospect that she spent two hours perfecting her toilet.

Sarah and Eleanor and their devoted maid Mary Carryl were buried together in St Collen's churchyard in Llangollen, in a grave marked by a three-sided monument. Mary died in 1809, Eleanor in 1829 and Sarah in 1831.

FIG.15 Sarah Ponsonby (left) and Lady Eleanor Butler, known as the Ladies of Llangollen, with a dog, by J.H. Lynch, after Mary Parker (1828). *Wellcome Collection*

TEN

THE ABDUCTION CLUBS OF IRELAND

GARRET BYRNE, JAMES STRANGE & THE KENNEDY SISTERS

> Kilkenny, October 18. Saturday last our assizes ended, when the following persons received sentence, viz. in the county court, Gerald [sic] Byrne, Patrick Strange and James Strange, found guilty of feloniously taking and carrying away Miss Catherine and Miss Anne Kennedy, with an intent that said Gerald Byrne and James Strange should marry them, to be hanged on Saturday the 2d of December next.
>
> *Saunders's News-Letter, 20 October 1780*

ALTHOUGH THE PREMISE of the 2002 film *The Abduction Club*, in which a group of Irish noblemen kidnap girls in order to marry into their fortune sounds far-fetched, it was indeed based on a real phenomenon – the kidnapping of Irish heiresses by squireens, the younger sons of genteel families. These young men were additionally disadvantaged by their Catholicism, which excluded them from civil or military posts. The formal existence of 'clubs' has not been proven but abductions of unmarried women in Ireland tended to follow a pattern: the girl was snatched from home at night, sometimes violently, by armed men; she was sometimes dragged from her bed in her nightclothes, thrown across a horse and carried off to the hills or some wild, isolated location. Here she was either raped or married forcibly and clandestinely. *The Abduction Club* was billed as a rom-com, but the reality was anything but.

Garret Byrne (not Gerald as *Saunders's News-Letter* had it) of Ballyaun in County Carlow and James Strange of Ullard in County Kilkenny were well known as 'dissipated, dashing, careless, spirited fellows'. Byrne was said to have formed a romantic attachment to his cousin Catherine Kennedy, the fifteen-year-old daughter of Richard Kennedy of Raithmeaden in Waterford, who, like her fourteen-year-old sister Anne, was entitled in their father's will to £2,000, which was a huge sum in Ireland at that time.[51]

As a family member, Byrne escorted the sisters to social events and he often did so accompanied by his friend James Strange. According to the historian Margery Weiner,[52] in April 1779, Byrne and Strange became enraged after they turned up late at a dance in Graiguenamanagh in County Kilkenny and found the sisters dancing with other men. A week later Catherine, Anne and their mother were spending an evening at the home of a friend when the door was broken down and a crowd of armed men, including Strange's brother Patrick, rushed in. The two Kennedy girls were thrown over horses ridden by Byrne and Strange and taken off, first of all to a house at Kilmacshane, near Inistiogue where they firmly rejected any idea of marriage. However, hauled from place to place, their resistance eventually worn to shreds by threats, they gave in, and a priest was produced. He was probably a 'couple-beggar', a mendicant or migratory friar or priest willing to perform clandestine marriages. After the ceremony the men went drinking and, when they returned, raped their new 'wives'.

Prompted by the girls' distraught mother, the Lord Lieutenant of Ireland, Lord Lifford, issued a proclamation offering a hundred pounds for the apprehension and successful prosecution of Byrne, the Stranges and their accomplices. The General Association of Wexford, assisted by the military, leapt into action.

Byrne and the Strange brothers were now wanted men and went on the run. They had believed that once married to the girls they would be welcomed back into the family fold. Instead, they had no option but to leave Ireland and, with the girls, headed for Rush, County Dublin, for the boat to Bordeaux where there was an Irish community including relatives who might offer refuge. However, when their vessel stopped off at Wicklow and Garret Byrne and Strange went ashore for supplies, leaving the Kennedy girls with Patrick Byrne, the authorities boarded the boat and the girls rescued.

Byrne and Strange next fled to Wales but were captured and returned to Kilkenny, where they were put on trial for their lives. Catherine and Anne appeared in court, facing down the abductors with whom they had been forced to cohabit and have sex while they were fugitives and who still asserted that they were their husbands. Letters purporting to be from the sisters, in which they invited the men to carry them off, were proved to be forgeries concocted by Anne Byrne. Other letters, in which the Kennedy sisters wrote affectionately of Byrne and Strange and called them their 'dear husbands', had clearly been written under duress. After a seventeen-hour hearing, the jury retired and two hours later returned a verdict of Guilty with a strong recommendation to mercy.

After the trial was over, a mob hurled insults and threats at the Kennedy sisters, who, guarded by Volunteers, were driven back to Rathmaiden. Byrne and the Strange brothers were returned to gaol to await hanging. Could they be rescued? It was not unknown for mobs to liberate felons from ill-guarded lock-ups. In 1779, James Caar was sprung on his way to his execution for helping his friend Thomas Condron in 'ravishing' Judith Kitchell, who had been feloniously carried away without her consent.[53]

One of the many interesting features of this episode is the esteem in which Byrne and Strange were held by ordinary people. The men were admired as gentlemen who had married the Kennedy girls rather than simply raping them, and abduction was not seen as a particularly serious crime, so many of their supporters were astonished that their capital sentences were not commuted.

Sympathies were not confined to Ireland. *The Derby Mercury* was of the opinion that the sentence was excessive.

> At the same Time that we acknowledge the Propriety of the Law, and the necessity of its rigid Execution, in a County said to be more remarkable for such Outrage than any other Part of the Kingdom; yet it should be remembered the unhappy Culprits were not vulgar Ruffians, but Gentlemen of irreproachable Characters, of equal Birth and Connection with their Prosecutors.[54]

FIG.16 A Trial for a Rape by an unknown artist (1799). The victim in this satirical print has been labelled 'Hibernica' (Ireland). Although the subject is political, it reflects contemporary attitudes to accusations of rape. The observers' comments include 'he must have been drunk at the time' and 'a pretty heaven born spark to be sure to want to violate a woman against her will'.
Yale Center for British Art, Paul Mellon Collection, B1981.25.1663

Byrne and Strange had merely miscalculated that 'certain Reconciliation, as a natural Consequence, would immediately follow the Deed, as the intimacy grew up from a state of Nonage to that of Maturity'.

The place of execution at Kilkenny, a mile from the gaol, was heavily guarded on 2 December 1780 when Byrne, the Strange brothers and another felon, Michael Brenan, who had been condemned for stealing a bullock, were brought out. The mob pelted the hangman with stones. Brenan was cut down after an hour. Then it was the turn of the three abductors. They emerged, each wearing white satin breeches and waistcoats, with Byrne in an emerald green coat, James Strange in light blue and Patrick in mulberry, flanked by priests and surrounded by sheriff's men. After the hanging their bodies were given to their families for burial. Hostility towards the Kennedy sisters became visceral. They were hissed, booed and harassed in public, and despite subsequently marrying respectably both died in misery. This was seen as a just ending for their treachery, the vengeance of Heaven.[55]

By the end of the eighteenth century, abduction in England was rare. In Ireland, however, while it could not be said to be common, it happened with much greater frequency. According to Margery Weiner writing in 1968, this was partly because of the persistence of a folk tradition of forcible marriage, conducted when 'the local peasantry decided that it was time a particular girl was rescued from spinsterhood'. The girl was informed that on the following Sunday she would be 'horsed' (carried on a young man's back), after which there would be a part,y including a hurling match, with the winner taking her as a bride.

For the squireens, unemployed, aspirational, often with dissipated habits, forcible marriage was a viable option and capital punishment must have seemed an unlikely outcome. Abductors featured in the culture of the street:

I am a bold undaunted youth,
My name is John McCann.
I'm a native of old Donegal,
Convenient to Strabane.
For the stealing of an heiress
I lie in Lifford Jail,
The father swears he'll hang me
For his daughter, Mary Neill.[56]

One of the most famous incidents was the abduction in 1772 of wealthy heiress Charlotte Newcomen of Carrigglas, County Longford by Thomas Johnston. Charlotte was staying in Longford with her elderly guardian Mr. Shepherd when Johnston, the son of a respectable yeoman farmer, together with a gang of helpers, marched up to the house, seized and bound the old man, and dashed up to Charlotte's bedroom.

> Miss Newcomen... made all the resistance that woman could do. She was dragged downstairs. On the first flight Miss Webster met her and caught her in her arms, then both held fast by the banister of the stair. Johnston, they say, cried out 'Break their arms!'... As Johnston came out of the door, a Miss Cornwell, niece to Mr. Webster, who lived next door, struck him on the head with an iron pin which fastened his window...
>
> The poor soul [Miss Newcomen]... scratched Johnston's face, cuffed Edwards, tore his hair, and kept herself so still by the help of an iron that was to the pillion, that they could not get her fixed to the horse, though they... dragged [her] barefoot through a street dirty as possible, and in their attempts to put her on horseback used her with as much roughness and as little delicacy as if she had been a common hussy.[57]

Johnston did not get very far. Some reports say that Mr. Shepherd, released from his ropes, shot one of the gang with a blunderbuss, others that it was his outraged son. Either way, one of the gang died, and Johnston was later executed at the gallows.

Charlotte, who was engaged to a wealthy Dublin banker at the time, had earlier in the day danced with Johnston at a party given for the tenantry. She went on to marry her fiancé but she never fully recovered from the shock of the events at Longford. According to an obituary of her son, Lord Viscount Newcomen, 'The melancholy catastrophe permanently depressed her spirits.'

ELEVEN

THE MISER'S GRANDDAUGHTER

EMILY ELWES & THOMAS DUFFIELD

Author and historian JOANNE MAJOR tells the tangled tale of Emily Elwes, born into a notoriously miserly family, who set her heart on marrying Oxford fellow Thomas Duffield

AMELIA MARIA FRANCES ELWES, known as Emily, was the only child, and heir, of George Elwes of Marcham Park in Berkshire,[58] and Portman Square in London. The newspapers were probably over-egging the pudding when they reported in 1810 that she stood to inherit more than a million pounds.[59] Whatever the true extent of her fortune, she was certainly going to be a very wealthy woman. Of course, with that kind of money, Emily was not short of suitors but her heart had already been captured. She was in love with a man named Thomas Duffield.

George Elwes owed his immense fortune to the parsimony of his father, John. Known as both an eccentric and a miser, John Elwes was born John Meggot (or Meggott), the son of a successful Southwark brewer. After a classical education at Westminster School, John embarked on a Grand Tour of Europe's major cities during which he met the philosopher Voltaire and gained a reputation as one of the best horsemen in Europe. He inherited his father's substantial fortune as well that of his uncle, Sir Hervey Elwes, 2nd Baronet of Stoke-by-Clare, Suffolk (John took his uncle's surname in order to inherit). Once in possession of all that money, John took great care not to part with it.

Parsimony ran in the family. Sir Hervey Elwes had also been described as a miser, and it may have been his influence that steered John on the path that would come to define his life: penny-pinching to the extreme. It is believed that he was Charles Dickens's inspiration for Ebenezer Scrooge.

It becomes difficult to separate fact from fiction when it comes to John Elwes's life. He was said to wear rags and a wig discarded by a beggar. His fine Georgian mansion, Marcham Park, became so dilapidated that during heavy showers water poured through the ceilings. When travelling, he was reluctant to spend money on food and instead carried hardboiled eggs in his pocket.

Although he never married, John had two illegitimate sons who each gained a portion of his fortune. One of those sons was George Elwes, Emily's father, who inherited Marcham Park. He married Amelia Maria Alt in 1789 and Emily, their only child, was born two years later.

What of Emily's suitor? Thomas Duffield was born in 1782, the son of Michael Duffield of Syston near Grantham in Lincolnshire. He gained his bachelor's degree at Christ Church, Oxford in 1804, and then studied for a Master of Arts at Merton College, after which, from 1807 until 1811, he was a fellow at Merton.

At first, George Elwes allowed Thomas to 'pay his addresses' to his daughter, but 'some changes in the opinions of the governing part of the family had arisen, and other suitors were strongly recommended to the young lady'. Emily had other ideas, however, and she did not lack determination.

Thomas was barred from the Elwes' house, but this did not keep him away. He and two friends hatched a plan with, it seems, Emily's knowledge and consent. In the first weeks of 1810, while her mother had a female friend staying with her, one of Thomas's co-conspirators contrived to be invited into the Elwes family home where he pretended to be this unnamed lady's suitor and future husband. One morning in early February, Mrs. Elwes and her friend were persuaded to go shopping together. No sooner had they left than a chaise and four drew up to the house.

George Elwes bumped into his daughter as she was walking to the front door with Thomas's friend. When he asked where they were off to, Emily said she was just 'going to her mamma, who was waiting for her'. Mr Elwes had no reason to doubt his daughter — Emily was not wearing a hat and was not dressed for an outing. There was no suspicion that she was about to flee her home.

Emily was handed into the waiting chaise. Inside was Thomas Duffield, ready to spirit her away. His job completed, Thomas's friend strolled back into the house. When Mr. Elwes asked where Emily was, the friend replied that she had been delivered 'to the man destined to make her happy; and that she was off to Gretna Green'.

Chaos ensued. Servants were sent to find Mrs. Elwes, who returned home in a panic. Emily's parents raced northwards but, having reached St. Albans with no sight of their daughter, gave up and returned home. As Thomas and Emily headed for the Scottish border, the newspapers picked up the story.

> An elopement has taken place, which will make a very considerable noise. The elegant Miss Elwes... eloped with a young clergyman of Oxford [Oxford University later denied he was ordained], of the name of Duffield... She is under age, but was not made a Ward of Chancery.[60]

The couple reached Gretna Green where Thomas paid fifty pounds to 'old Parson Joseph' (Joseph Paisley), of whom it was said that he drank 'nothing but brandy, and has neither been sick nor sober these forty years', to marry them.

With the deed done, George Elwes had no choice but to make the best of things. He insisted that his daughter and new son-in-law go through a second marriage ceremony, just to be sure things were legal and above board, and this took place a month later at St. Marylebone church in London. In time, he was reconciled with his daughter and grew to be fond of Thomas.

However, the story did not end there. In October 1802, George Elwes signed a settlement that conveyed real estates upon trust for the benefit of his daughter but also declared that if she married under age or without his consent the trustees should hold the estates in trust for him and his heirs.

Emily was eighteen and therefore a minor when she married and

FIG.17 John Elwes 'was a man respecting himself of an extraordinary penurious and singular turn'. *Wellcome Collection, 288i*

FIG.18 The church at St. Marylebone by James Miller (date unknown), where Emily Elwes and Thomas Duffield were married for the second time. *Yale Center for British Art, Gift of Paul Mellon in memory of Dudley Snelgrove, B1993.30.107(10)*

she certainly went through the Gretna wedding ceremony without her father's consent. After that, however, Thomas had been accepted as part of the family and was even given possession of the Elwes' mansion.

George died in 1821 and left a legal mess. Although he had said, in the clearest terms, that he wanted Emily and Thomas Duffield to inherit his estates, he had neglected to revoke the earlier settlement. Emily's widowed mother made a second marriage to William Hicks, after which she and her new husband contested George Elwes' will. It became a protracted and complicated case, but the Duffields eventually managed to retain their rights to Marcham Park.[61]

Emily and her mother then put all their disagreements behind them. Amelia Hicks's will, written in 1824, left her daughter and her Duffield grandchildren many personal bequests. Perhaps it was Mr. Hicks who was the driving force behind the legal battles.

After bearing three sons and six daughters, Emily Duffield died in 1835 at the age of forty-three, and was buried at All Saints church in Marcham. Thomas, who was MP for Abingdon between 1832 and 1844, married for a second time, to Augusta Rushbrooke by whom he had four further children. By the time of his death, in 1854, he was living at The Priory in Wallingford, Oxfordshire, and his son by Emily, Charles Philip Duffield, inhabited Marcham Park.

TWELVE

'WE FLY BY NIGHT'

MARY BURTON & WILLIAM FIELDS

JOANNE MAJOR's story of the elopement of the daughter of a miller with a linen draper is evidence that fugitive marriage affected families of all ranks and also illustrates the fragility of women's lives

AT AROUND MIDNIGHT, Mary Burton crept out of her father's house into William Fields' arms. He had a carriage waiting for her, and together the couple fled into the frosty landscape. *The Stamford Mercury*'s headline, on 4 December 1812, described their elopement in poetic terms: 'WE FLY BY NIGHT... on the wings of love.'

It might be a slight disappointment, after imagining the Regency-era lovebirds speeding through the midnight hours, to find that their destination was nowhere glamorous. They travelled forty miles to William's home in Kingston upon Hull on the northern bank of the Humber Estuary, in East Yorkshire.

Six years earlier, in 1806, the English dramatist George Colman the Younger's two-act musical farce *We Fly by Night; or, Long Stories*[62] in which an elopement forms the central plot, premiered at Covent Garden before going on tour around the country. Two years later, the play was performed in front of a full house at Hull's Theatre Royal.[63] Perhaps

FIG.19 The harbour at Hull, Yorkshire by an unknown artist (1814). The city was a busy international trading hub.
Yale Center for British Art, Paul Mellon Collection. B1975.3.384

FIG.20 The well-known linen drapers Harding, Howell & Co. of Pall Mall, London. William Field's establishment in Kingston upon Hull would have been similar but on a more modest scale. From Rudolph Ackermann, *The Repository of arts, literature, commerce, manufactures, fashions and politics* (1809).
Wikimedia Commons

William Fields was in the audience that evening and remembered the storyline. *The Stamford Mercury*'s reporter was clearly aware of it when he wrote the headline.

In the play, the young girl's father is a high-ranking military officer. Mary Burton's family was more prosaic. Her father was a miller and baker who lived in Gainsborough in Lincolnshire, and Mary was his only daughter. The morning following the elopement, when Mr. Burton discovered that Mary was missing, he guessed straight away where she had gone and set off for Hull in hot pursuit.

The wedding ceremony was carried out at Hull's Holy Trinity Church on 25 November 1812,[64] the day the couple arrived in the city. William Fields, who had procured a marriage licence in advance, had planned the elopement with care. Mary's father arrived too late to prevent it. In any case, Mary was over twenty-one and therefore did not need her parents' permission to marry.[65]

William Fields was a linen draper, trading as one half of Everington and Fields of Kingston upon Hull. Less than a month after William and Mary's marriage, the partnership was dissolved and William carried on the business alone, promising to pay all debts owed.[66] He operated from 9 Whitefriargate, in the heart of the city, close to the docks in what is now Hull's most historic street. At the time William and Mary Fields lived there, probably above the drapery business, its private houses had been converted into shops. There were also several inns, and stables housing stallions destined for export by sea.

Cragg's Guide to Hull of 1817[67] describes the main streets of the city as 'broad and airy; in the middle, they are formed commodiously for carriages, and, at the sides, conveniently for foot passengers: and the whole town is well paved, flagged, and lighted. The population... in 1811, amounted to thirty-eight thousand.'

Hull's dockland was expanding, and the city sat at the heart of a thriving trading network, both coastal, inland, and overseas. Trade routes included the East Indies and the Baltics, and whaling and fishing were major industries. Cragg pointed out that Hull's proximity to Yorkshire's manufacturing districts led it to be 'in the first class of mercantile towns'. William Fields had every opportunity to make a success of his drapery business and he needed to do so as it wasn't long before Mary was pregnant.

Just over a year after the wedding, William Fields found himself the father of William Burton Fields, who was baptised in Hull on 11 January 1814. On the same day, William also attended the burial of his wife. Mary had died in childbirth, aged just twenty-two.

In the parish register entry for his son's christening, William gave his occupation as 'grocer'. All became clear a few weeks later. In February 1814, William announced his change of career by informing the readers of the *Hull Packet* newspaper that he had taken the grocery shop at 3 North Bridge, Witham.[68] These new premises were further from the centre of the city. There, customers could purchase tea, coffee, spices, and sugar, commodities no doubt brought into Hull's docks on East Indiamen ships.

After Mary's death, this was a new beginning. However, whatever other qualities William Fields had, success in business was not one of them. By the end of 1815, William was bankrupt.[69] Perhaps his father-in-law was right in his initial judgment of his hapless son-in-law.

Mary and William's son died, aged just eleven, on 27 December 1825 in Gainsborough and was buried two days later at All Saints, a beautiful eighteenth-century church modelled on London's St. Martin-in-the-Fields.[70] That he was laid to rest in Gainsborough and not alongside his mother in Hull suggests that young William was living with, or visiting, his maternal grandfather when he fell ill.

The Stamford Mercury's 1812 headline invoking the title of a farce could not have ended up being further from the truth. Mary Burton and William Fields' elopement, carried out with so much hope, ended in terrible tragedy.

THIRTEEN

'THIS LOVE HATH TURN'D THY BRAIN'

RICHARD BRINSLEY SHERIDAN & ELIZABETH LINLEY

JOANNE MAJOR tells the story of the elopement of celebrated soprano Elizabeth Linley with playwright Richard Sheridan who went on to use some of its elements – rescue from forced marriage, a night-time flight to the Continent and a furious and greedy parent – in his works for the stage[71]

ELIZABETH ANN LINLEY was born into a musical family in Bath in 1754. Her father Thomas was a composer, singer and music teacher and her mother's talents were reckoned equal to his. The family was a large one, with Elizabeth the eldest of twelve, eight of whom survived into adulthood, of whom seven, including Elizabeth, embarked on musical or theatrical careers.

As a child, Elizabeth performed on stage and in 1787, at the age of thirteen, made her Covent Garden debut. She was primarily known as a soprano, but there was more to her than that. She was also a poet and writer, and a noted bluestocking, one of a group of women interested in discussing literary and philosophical subjects.

She was also beautiful and did not lack suitors. The Linley family, however talented, was impoverished, and Elizabeth's father arranged a match for her to wealthy sixty-year-old Walter Long, who showered her with gifts, including jewellery. At around this time, the theatrical Sheridan family moved to Bath. Dublin-born and Harrow-educated, Richard Brinsley Sheridan was twenty and a budding playwright. His sister, Alicia, three years his junior, became firm friends with Elizabeth Linley.[72]

Elizabeth's engagement to Long had not gone unnoticed by the world at large. The actor and dramatist Samuel Foote mocked both parties in his play *The Maid of Bath*, which premiered in 1771 at the Haymarket Theatre in London and ran for over three weeks. Long was satirised as Solomon Flint and Elizabeth as Kitty Linnet. This might be the reason Long broke off the engagement, or he may have been concerned that other men were showing too much interest in his bride-to-be. Also, Elizabeth was reported to have told Long that she would never be happy as his wife. Regardless of the cause of the break, he paid Elizabeth £3,000 in compensation and allowed her to keep his gifts.

The other men who pestered Elizabeth included Richard Sheridan's older brother Charles but the one who troubled her most was a married friend of her father's. Thomas Mathews styled himself as a captain who had resigned his military commission. In truth, he had never risen higher in rank than ensign and, although technically an officer, he was no gentleman. He harassed Elizabeth and threatened to rape her. She was driven to the brink of suicide before her friend Alicia Sheridan stepped in. The girls concocted a plan and decided that Elizabeth should flee to the safety of a French convent. Alicia involved her brother Richard in the scheme, unaware that he had developed a romantic attachment to Elizabeth.

On the morning of 18 March 1772, Elizabeth refused to get out of bed, pleading a headache. Alicia offered to sit by her bedside while the family were out performing at a concert. As soon as the Linleys left, Elizabeth packed her belongings and waited for Richard. Initially, the newspapers reported that the couple had eloped on a 'matrimonial expedition to Scotland', but in fact Richard and Elizabeth fled to London. From there they escaped to Dunkirk and went on towards Calais. Although the plan had ostensibly been to escort Elizabeth to a convent, Richard persuaded her that they should marry instead. No record of the ceremony has been found but it is reputed to have taken place towards the end of March at a village near Calais. However, the marriage would have been invalid as both Elizabeth and Richard were minors.

FIG.21 Elizabeth Linley, Mrs. Richard Brinsley Sheridan, by Thomas Gainsborough (c. 1775). As a noted beauty, Elizabeth was also painted by Joshua Reynolds.
The National Gallery of Art, Andrew W. Mellon Collection

The couple travelled to Lille, where Elizabeth became unwell, exhibiting the early symptoms of tuberculosis. Meanwhile, gossip circulated back home as news of the 'marriage' spread. The part played by Captain Mathews became known and he left Bath, although not before placing an advertisement in *The Bath Chronicle*:

> Mr. Richard S[heridan] having attempted, in a Letter left behind him for that Purpose, to account for his scandalous Method of running away from this Place, by Insinuations, derogating from *my* Character, and that of a young Lady, *innocent* as far as relates to *me* or my *Knowledge*... I can no longer think he deserves the Treatment of a Gentleman, and therefore shall trouble myself no further about him, than in this public Method to post him as a *L[iar]* and a treacherous *S[coundrel]*...[73]

Amongst all the commotion, Elizabeth's father went to France in search of his daughter. His primary concern was that Elizabeth had been contracted for performances and he stood to lose money if she failed to appear. After some persuading, Elizabeth returned but only after gaining promises that her workload would be reduced and that she would be allowed to go back to France.

Sheridan travelled with her and her father but, once in London, he slipped away, intent on finding Mathews. When he was cornered, Mathews claimed that Sheridan had been given false information about the *Bath Chronicle* advertisement. Sheridan let the matter rest but, as soon as he got back to Bath, he went to the newspaper office to check. He discovered that Mathews had not only been defamatory in print but had now compounded the insult by lying to Sheridan's face. Back to London went Sheridan and, this time, he challenged Mathews to a duel.

They fought by candlelight at the Castle Tavern on Soho's Henrietta Street. Mathews was disarmed and ended up begging for his life. Sheridan demanded he publish an apology:

> Being convinced that the Expressions I made Use of to Mr. Sheridan's Disadvantage, were the effects of Passion and Misrepresentation, I retract what I have said to that Gentleman's Disadvantage, and particularly beg his Pardon for my Advertisements in the Bath Chronicle. THOMAS MATHEWS.[74]

FIG.22 The playwright Richard Brinsley Sheridan by the studio of Joshua Reynolds (date unknown).
By kind permission of the Garrick Club

That should have been the end of the matter but Mathews then spread lies about his defeat and continued to berate Sheridan. The two men met again, at Kingsmead outside Bath, at dawn on 2 July. They were drunk. This time Mathews gained the upper hand after both of their swords broke and the duel descended into a brawl. Mathews repeatedly stabbed Sheridan, leaving him for dead but, thanks to the skill of local surgeons, he recovered.[75]

Both Elizabeth and Richard's parents opposed their relationship, and the star-crossed lovers were parted. Elizabeth received at least two further proposals of marriage, which were encouraged by her avaricious father, but she refused to countenance them. Then, in early 1773, Richard and Elizabeth were reunited. Sheridan was now twenty-one, and he convinced Elizabeth's father to allow them to marry. They wed, officially this time, at St. Marylebone Church on 13 April 1773.

Once Elizabeth was his wife, Sheridan would not allow her to appear on stage. He did, however, permit her to perform at their home, for which he charged admission, and when they were invited to stay at stately homes. Elizabeth, in effect, sang for their supper during the years that Sheridan was a struggling playwright but, by doing so became close friends with several aristocratic women, including Georgiana, Duchess of Devonshire. With her influence, Elizabeth became involved in politics, campaigning for the Whigs and supporting Charles James Fox, and Sheridan was elected MP for Stafford in 1780. He became a confidant of the Prince of Wales, later the Prince Regent.

Sheridan's career blossomed. His plays were successful, and he moved into theatre management, becoming the part-owner of Drury Lane's Theatre Royal together with his father-in-law and Dr. Ford. Two of Sheridan's plays, *The Rivals* (1775) and *The School for Scandal* (1777), include duelling scenes inspired by his own fights with Captain Mathews. Elizabeth played her part in supporting her husband, working behind the scenes to assist him. As a noted beauty, she was painted by the best artists of the day, including Thomas Gainsborough and Joshua Reynolds.

The Sheridans had a son, Tom, but Elizabeth suffered many miscarriages. The novelist Fanny Burney, writing of Elizabeth in 1779, claimed that the couple were 'extremely happy in each other; he evidently adores her, and she as evidently idolizes him.'[76] However, despite the romance of their marriage, it was not a success. They both took lovers and lived separate lives while putting on a united front at social events to avoid scandal. On 30 March 1792, Elizabeth gave birth to a short-lived daughter whose father was the Irish radical Lord Edward FitzGerald.

The tuberculosis from which Elizabeth had suffered for so long finally caught up with her. At Bristol Hotwells, less than three months after the birth of her daughter, she died aged thirty-eight, and was buried at Wells Cathedral.

Reports said that Sheridan was inconsolable but, later that year, both he and FitzGerald simultaneously fell in love with 'Pamela', the writer Madame de Genlis' mysterious adopted niece, who was rumoured to be the child of the Duc d'Orléans (Philippe Égalité) and reminded both men of Elizabeth. Engaged first to Sheridan, Pamela subsequently married FitzGerald on 27 December 1792. Sheridan made a second marriage in 1795, to nineteen-year-old Hester Jane (Hecca) Ogle, the daughter of the Dean of Winchester.

Richard Brinsley Sheridan's latter years were beset by debts and ill health. He died in poverty in 1815, although his funeral, held in Westminster Abbey's Poet's Corner, was attended by members of the nobility.

FOURTEEN

'THE LAST SOLACE OF MY LIFE'

MARCIA GRANT & BRINSLEY SHERIDAN

> I have found it hard, very hard, my Lord, to bear up against those afflictions which the will of Heaven has visited me with, till but only one of all I had to bless my home was left to me, it is, I find beyond humanity to endure that this last solace of my life, for whom alone I wished to live, should be torn from me by a train of artifice disgraceful as it is cruel.
>
> *Sir John Colquhoun Grant writing in The Morning Post, 30 May 1835*

FOR A FEW DAYS in the spring of 1835, 'the fashionable world was in ferment'[77] over the elopement of Marcia Grant, the twenty-year-old daughter and sole heir of the elderly Waterloo hero General Sir John Colquhoun Grant, with Brinsley Sheridan, the grandson of the playwright Richard Brinsley Sheridan.

The couple were said to have first met at the house of Brinsley Sheridan's sister, the celebrated author Caroline Norton. Sheridan had recently returned from service as a clerk in the East India Company. He had political ambitions (he was later a Whig Member of Parliament) but no resources. Marcia, by contrast, was reputed to have £40,000 of her own, and 'expectations of a considerable fortune in addition to this'[78] on the death of her father – plus a life interest in her father's magnificent mansion and estate at Frampton in Dorset.

On Friday 15 May 1835, Marcia used her father's absence from home — he was standing for Parliament in Poole — as an opportunity to escape her guardian Sir Robert Macfarlane, who had been entrusted by the General to keep an eye on her. In an archly-worded account, *The Staffordshire Advertiser* explained how the young couple escaped:

> On Friday week, about one o'clock, Mrs. Norton called, and took the young lady out for a drive in the Parks; and being there, by some unaccountable accident, her brother, Mr. Brinsley Sheridan, was there also and... could do no less than gallantly renew his attention to Miss Grant. Of course he obtained a seat in the same carriage. From the Park, they drove to another sister of Mrs. Norton, Lady Seymour. Here a scene occurred, which ended in... Sheridan borrowing from his friend Colonel Bentinck, of the Guards, the use of his travelling carriage, which had just driven up, of course by accident. There was no impediment to immediate elopement, but a wardrobe and money. The kind sisters supplied this between them, and in addition furnished a lady's maid. Miss Grant wrote a note to her own waiting woman, by way of ruse directing her to proceed with her wardrobe to Dover. All the preliminaries thus arranged, the parties popped into the carriage and were very soon in full swing for Gretna-Green.[79]

Marcia's hapless father pursued the couple to Kent, believing they were headed for Europe. It was a plot twist worthy of a grandson of Richard Sheridan, the author of *The Rivals* and *School for Scandal,* who as a young man had eloped with his eighteen-year-old lover, the beautiful Elizabeth Ann Linley (see page 77). Marcia and Brinsley arrived at Gretna Green after travelling for a straight thirty-two hours and married at five o'clock on Sunday morning.

As soon as Macfarlane was aware that Marcia had fled, he charged round to Brinsley Sheridan's sister Caroline Norton's house in Spring Gardens, where he found her, her husband George, her sister Lady Georgiana Seymour and her husband Lord Seymour, her sister the poet and composer Helen Blackwood, and her mother (another eloper in her youth).[80]

Caroline Norton refused to answer McFarlane's questions about who had abducted Marcia and where they had gone. Sir Colquhoun Grant, now incandescant with fury, accused George Norton and Lord Seymour of complicity, and couched his reproaches in terms of 'honour', 'disgrace' and 'satisfaction', a euphemistic challenge to a duel. George Norton, denying he had anything to do with the business, declined, sheltering behind his role as a public servant (he was a magistrate). Eventually, Sir Colquhoun Grant accepted his plea of ignorance about the plan.

Lady Seymour also refused to answer Sir Colquhoun Grant's questions, prompting another challenge. This time, it was answered and Lord Seymour met him at dawn on Hampstead Heath, where they discharged their arms. Both misssed their target and Seymour's second persuaded him to offer an explanation of his part in the affair.

Sir Colquhoun Grant took legal action against Brinsley Sheridan, forcing him to return from honeymoon in Cumberland to answer a criminal summons in the Court of Chancery in London — Marcia was still a minor and her father alleged she had been abducted.

It is difficult not to have sympathy for Sir Colquhoun Grant. He was, in the words he used in a widely published letter to Seymour, in an 'agony of mind'; he had not been able to 'calm my senses, or command my reason.' Marcia was 'the only remaining prop and comfort of my life'. He had come to fatherhood in his late forties. His wife had died in 1818, his son Francis at the age of ten, and his daughter Charlotte at the age of sixteen, only two years before Marcia's elopement. He had shown the most astonishing endurance and bravery on the battlefield at Waterloo — five horses had been shot out from under him and he had been wounded — but he was felled by his emotions.

Meanwhile, the press was taking delight in cryptic references to the 'bride's nightcap', which may have been veiled hints at the scandalous affair between Caroline Norton and the Prime Minister, Lord Melbourne.[81]

In June, Marcia and Brinsley married again, this time at Arthuret in Cumberland. By September, Sir Colquhoun Grant, previously so full of heat and rage, had rethought his situation. In a piece titled 'The Calm After the Tempest', the *Court Journal* noted that he had left London for Frampton in the company of Mr. and Mr. Sheridan.[82] He died there in

December 1835, after a short illness, with his daughter and son-in-law at his side, fully reconciled.

Brinsley Sheridan's political career gained momentum, and he was elected member of parliament first for Shaftesbury and then for Dorchester. He and Marcia cultivated a circle of literary friends, including William Makepeace Thackerary and Mary Shelley. They had nine children. Marcia died in 1882 and Brinsley in 1888.

FIFTEEN

ELOPEMENT IN THE NEWS

THIS SELECTION OF newspaper reports from 1759 to 1837 show the wide range of treatments of the subject of elopement in the news media. It comes with a health warning: nothing should be taken at face value. However, where I have been able to verify the identity of protagonists I have done so and in a few cases I have tracked their stories through other sources.

The only change to the text I have made is to alter the following *l.* in sums of money to the pound symbol (£). Grammar and spelling, not at that time fully regularised, are as they appeared in the original. Occasionally I have given [sic] for clarification. I have also included indications of the locations of streets and towns.

1759

A Gentleman of Distinction has eloped with his Mother's Chambermaid, and Yesterday several Persons were in Search after him. *Oxford Journal, 3 February 1759*

1760

The two Persons of Distinction, who some Time since made an Elopement, with a Design of going to Scotland to be married, but were stopt in their Progress, it is said, are likely to have their Wishes soon completed, by the Consent of both Families.

Oxford Journal, 9 February 1760

A young Lady of Family and Fortune, near Chippenham in Wiltshire, of about 19 Years of Age, has lately eloped with her Father's Coachman. *Newcastle Courant, 30 August 1760*

The following account of the lady who lately eloped has been transmitted to the Printer of one of the Morning Papers:

"On Wednesday the 1st of October, four persons came to an English house in Rotterdam; a man of about five and forty years of age; a genteel young lad, who he calls, and who appears to be, his son; a young lady who came over to be married to this lad, very short, her age supposed to be about sixteen, her name Patty: the fourth person was a woman of middling stature, thin, and remarkable for having large fore-teeth, her name Kitty. The laws of the country do not allow of any persons being married without having their banns publickly asked, and if they are strangers, a certificate of their friends consent besides. This has frustrated their whole scheme; they cannot be married here. They are afraid of going to a Roman Chatholic [sic] country, for fear the marriage should not be valid. They thought once of going to a town in the Prince of Orange's domain; but that scheme is, I believe, at an end, by their being very short of money. They will, in all probability, return to England by the packet. If her friends are desirous of recovering her, their best way will be to go and wait for her at Harwich. The young lady seems at times to be in great uneasiness, and heartily sorry for the folly she has been guilty of; at other times pretty chearful, as they take great pains to amuse her, and keep up her spirits.

"P.S. In case they do not go back so soon as is expected, her friends should take measures to have her secured here."

The young girl who has eloped from her friends to Holland, in order to be married, as mentioned in the first page of this paper, proves to be a young Lady of considerable fortune, and a ward of the Court of Chancery; and not above 16 years of age.

Leeds Intelligencer, 28 October 1760

1761

A young Lady of great Fortune eloped on Tuesday with her Father's Coachman. They are gone, it is supposed, for Scotland, to be married. *Bath Chronicle and Weekly Gazette, 29 January 1761*

It is reported that a young lady posses'd of a very large Fortune, made an Elopement last Monday Morning from her Friends, with a Banker's Clerk of this City. It is said that their first Interview was at Westminster on the Coronation Day.

Ipswich Journal, 3 October 1761

A young Lady, Daughter to an eminent Attorney near the Royal Exchange, lately made an Elopement from her Friends, with an Usher at an Academy, to Scotland, where they were married, and are since returned, and Matters are compromised to the Satisfaction of her Friends. *Ipswich Journal, 10 October 1761*

FIG.23 Satirical print published in 1791 illustrating the familiar elements of an elopement including the military suitor, home-loving bride-to-be, complicit maid and the waiting carriage. By the standards of the day the couple are old and physically ill-matched. Unknown artist.
Yale Center for British Art, Paul Mellon Collection, B1981.25.1693

1762

The following particulars concerning the lady, who lately put an end to her life, may be acceptable of our readers: About three months ago, a cornet of horse [cavalryman] went to her fathers [sic], a Hamborough merchant [sic – the Hambroughs were merchant adventurers] at Northaw [Hertfordshire], to ask the character of a servant, he not being home, the officer was introduced to the young lady, his daughter, who happened to be at tea. She gave the servant a fair character and after some chat, with the officer, asked him to drink a dish of tea: Thus began an acquaintance which the cornet cultivated by means of letters delivered by the servant. The lady it is said was an heiress to £30,000. The cornet declared himself to be the son of a country gentleman of fortune; but lest enquiries not prove in his favour he soon after insisted, that the lady should make an elopement, and be married at Barnet [north of London]. To run away was very disagreeable, and it was with much difficulty she was prevailed on. When they came to Barnet, where he was stationed, a mistake appearing in the licence, the cornet took horse and rode to London, and returned to Barnet time enough to be married which was done in the presence of a number of people. The young lady's mother soon reconciled to the match, but the father, who had proposed a more fortunate one for his daughter, refused to see her. The lady and the Cornet's friends used all practicable means to bring about a reconciliation, which the young lady despairing of seeing ever brought about, unhappily put an end to her life. *Leicester Journal, 23 January 1762*

1763

Monday the first Division of Lord Robert Manners's Regiment marched out of Chatham Barracks [in Kent] for their Quarters in Gloucester. The same morning a young Lady of great Beauty and Fortune (Miss O——e) eloped from her Friends, and was carried off by an Officer in the above Regiment (Captain Ch——r) towards the North. Miss O——e caused the

FIG.24 Student and Music Teacher, by Constantin Guys (unknown date, 19th century). Women's isolation within the home made them vulnerable to intense friendships with servants and tutors.
Yale University Art Gallery

following Letter to be delivered to her Mamma, some Hours after her Escape.

"By this time I am many Miles from my dear Mamma, and indeed I can't help wishing to be still farther from her, that my dear Ch—r may have it in his Power to make me his forever, which would never have happened with your Consent. I am sorry to have acted in this contrary to your Will, but there are Allowances to be made which I hope will plead my Excuse – I mean my utter Aversion to Mr. L—w (who you would have obliged me to marry) and my greatest Regard for Mr. Ch—r, who, I suppose, you wou'd oblige me not to marry; but indeed, my Mamma, 'tis now too late, for I will and must be his, though all the Powers were to oppose it. I am, my dear Mamma's very dutiful Daughter (though am afraid she will not think me so).

Chatham, Aug. 1, 1763. L— O—e.

P.S. Please to give my Love to my Sister, and tell her, if she expects to be happy, elope." *Derby Mercury, 5 August 1763*

A young Lady of great Fortune has eloped from the Care of an old Guardian to the Embraces of a young Lover, who conducted her to Jersey, where Marriage was solemnized, for which she has assigned her Guardian two powerful Reasons, Love and Freedom, without considering, that Marriage is but changing of Hands, and not launching into unlimited Licence.

Newcastle Courant, 6 August 1763

Last Friday a young Lady, of £15,000 Fortune, made an Elopement with a Gentleman of the Army (who lodged near Charing-Cross [London]) towards Scotland. The Gentleman had the Consent of several of her Relations; but it seems the Mother of the young Lady, not being altogether pleased, was full four Hours too late in her Pursuit to stop their Decampment.

Derby Mercury, 30 September 1763

A few Days since a young Lady of Fortune eloped from a Village near London, with a young Gentleman, for Edinburgh. What made the Case remarkable, was, that the young Gentleman visited the young Lady with Consent of her Mother and Friends, and was to have been soon married to her. But the Lady having a romantick Turn, would be run away with, and her Admirer consented to it, to prevent her requesting it from any one else. On their Return, their Friends shewed a proper Dislike to what she had done, and have insisted on her being married in England, as they are not satisfied with the Scotch Junction.

Oxford Journal, 19 November 1763

1764

Tuesday Evening a young Lady, who, when at Age, will have a fortune of upwards of Twenty Thousand Pounds, eloped with a Clergyman. She went from her Guardian's about Four o'Clock, in order to go the Play; but it is thought they went away directly for Scotland, her Guardian receiving a Letter from her the next Morning, in which were these Words: "Love has the Wings of a Dove, and I shall be got too far to be overtaken." We hear they took fresh Horses at Barnet at Six o'Clock, for St. Alban's.

Derby Mercury, 13 January 1764

We hear from Dover, that one of the Guardians to a Kentish Lady, who lately eloped, hearing she was gone thither to embark for France, pursued her last Sunday, and being informed that she had walked with her Spark towards the Hill, he sent several Persons to find her, which could not be effected; but instead of the young Lady sought after, another Couple in the same Circumstances, from Cuckfield in Sussex, were found near a Place called Lawless-church and conducted into Town; but being brought before the said Gentleman, were discharged, the lady not being the Person wanted; and the Couple embarked for France soon after.

Newcastle Courant, 30 June 1764

Tuesday last a young Lady of Fortune, who had eloped the Evening before, was overtaken by her Guardian a little beyond Barnet, on the Road to Scotland, concealed in a Mourning Hearse. The Lover, who is said to be a Military Gentleman, acted Coachman on the Occasion, disguised like an Undertaker. The disappointed Hero was suffered to depart, but the young Lady, with great Reluctance, returned to Town with her Guardian.

Derby Mercury, 21 December 1764

1765

The Daughter of a very eminent Personage has lately eloped, as we are informed, with a Black, who lived for some Years as Footman to her Father. *Derby Mercury, 5 April 1765*

A young Lady, Daughter to an eminent Merchant in this City [Oxford], falling in Love with her Father's Clerk, which being discovered, she was sent into the Country, and he was discharged; but the Gentleman having a Regard for the young Man, procured him a place of £100 a year; however the said young Lady finding herself disappointed of her Lover, took an Opportunity, in the Absence of her waiting Maid, to cut the arteries of her left Arm with a pair of Scissars [sic], which caused so great an Effusion of Blood, that she was just expiring before the Servant found it out: a Surgeon was immediately sent for, by whose care she recovered; soon after, the indulgent Father applied the properest method to make his Child happy, consented to their Marriage, and has given them a Fortune of £3000. *Oxford Journal, 6 April 1765*

The eldest son of a great family, a youth of eighteen, has, we hear, lately eloped to Scotland, with his mother's maid.

Leeds Intelligencer, 7 May 1765

Thursday Night the daughter of an eminent Citizen eloped with her Father's Clerk, and is supposed to have taken the Road to Edinburgh. The young Lady has an independent Fortune of £10,000 and the Lover is a very likely Fellow from Dublin.

Derby Mercury, 21 June 1765

We hear that a young Lady of considerable fortune (daughter-in-law [stepdaughter] to an eminent Pewterer in this city [Bath]) has lately elop'd from her uncle's seat at Blagdon in Somersetshire, with a young Farmer of that neighbourhood. It is suppos'd they are gone for Scotland to be married.

Bath Chronicle and Weekly Gazette, 25 July 1765

A young Lady, of immense Fortune, we hear, has eloped with her Father's French Valet; being traced a considerable Way on the Northern Road, it is imagined she intends to celebrate her nuptials in Edinburgh.

Bath Chronicle and Weekly Gazette, 22 August 1765

On Sunday last a young Lady, in Oxford road, heiress, to a very large fortune, eloped with a Player [actor]; it is imagined they are set out for North Britain, in order to enter into the bonds of Hymen. *Caledonian Mercury, 7 October 1765*

A short time since a young gentleman and lady of a large fortune eloped from their friends in town to an obscure village, some miles distant, where they took a lodging at the Clergyman's house of the parish, for one month, conformable to the late marriage act; but the young couple, being impatient to have the ceremony performed, persuaded the Parson to marry them some days before the time expired, for which an action is going to be commenced against him, for acting in open violation of the act. *Caledonian Mercury, 14 December 1765*

FIG.25 A courting or possibly an eloping couple in a chaise and pair, with post-boy, by Samuel Howitts. Undated.
Yale Center for British Art, Paul Mellon Collection. B2001.2.936

1766

They write from Edinburgh, that the young Lady from London, who made an Elopement with a journeyman Tailor last Year, but repented of her Frolic when she got to Newcastle, where she met with very inhospitable Treatment, and afterwards was sent back to her Friends, has, last week, made a second elopement with a Weaver, who her Friends have been told has a wife and children.

Oxford Journal, 19 July 1766

The Daughter of a Tradesman in the City [of London] was to have been married to an eminent Merchant, on Wednesday last, made an Elopement with her father's Journeyman, the very morning of her intended Nuptials.

Bath Chronicle and Weekly Gazette, 31 July 1766

Yesterday a young Lady of great Fortune eloped in a Post Chaise with her Father's Footman, from his House at Ilford [Essex]: the Father pursued them in a Post Chaise and Four, and came up with them at Mile End [east of London], but the Postilion dexterously drove down a by-lane and eluded their pursuer.

Oxford Journal, 30 August 1766

On Monday evening the Daughter of a reputable Tradesman of the Borough [in Southwark], and who is actually intitled to an independent Fortune of Six Thousand Pounds, on coming of Age, absconded from her Father's house, and one of the Clerks being missing, it is supposed that they are set out together for Scotland.

Oxford Journal, 30 August 1766

1767

We hear that on Thursday the daughter of a wealthy Jew, intitled to a very considerable fortune in her own right, and who lately turned Christian, eloped with a half-pay officer of the marines for Scotland. *Leeds Intelligencer, 2 June 1767*

We hear that on Monday evening a gentleman, who lived in Long Ditch [near St John's Street, London], poisoned himself. The cause of which is said to be his daughter's elopement with a footman, and carrying with her bank notes to the amount of £2000. *Kentish Gazette, 18 October 1767*

Last Week, a young Lady, Niece to an eminent Timber Merchant, with a Fortune of Ten Thousand Pounds at her own Disposal, eloped to Scotland with one of her Uncle's Clerks.

Oxford Journal, 31 October 1767

We are assured, that last Week a young Lady at the West End of the Town, who had a Fortune of £20,000 in her own Hands, married a young Fellow, whom she accidentally fell in Company with that Day, after no more than four Hours acquaintance.

Derby Mercury, 4 December 1767

1768

On Saturday last a young lady of great fashion made an elopement with her father's butler; she has £16,000 at her own disposal.

Kentish Gazette , 22 June 1768

A young lady of immense fortune eloped on Sunday last with her father's French valet; as they were seen in a post chariot on Shooter's Hill [Blackheath, south-east of London], it is conjectured that they are bound for France.

Oxford Journal, 23 July 1768

On Sunday last the heir to a title and large fortune eloped with the daughter of a taylor [sic], near Grosvenor Square [London], a girl of exquisite beauty. They are supposed to be gone to Scotland.

Bath Chronicle and Weekly Gazette, 4 August 1768

On Sunday last a poor curate in Berkshire married a young lady of immense fortune, without licence or publication of banns, to her father's groom. The priest is absconded to avoid the ceremony of being sent to the plantations. *Kentish Gazette, 15 October 1768*

Thursday a young lady of £12,000 fortune eloped to Scotland with a head waiter of a tavern in the City, carrying with her above £1000 in money and jewels. *Oxford Journal, 22 October 1768*

A few days ago the Daughter of an eminent Jew Merchant of this city [Oxford] eloped with a young Tradesman: the Lady has a large independent Fortune, which was lately left her by her Uncle, and it is supposed they are gone towards the North. The Gentleman has a Commission in the City Trained Bands, and it is imagined the Red Coat and gallant Appearance of this young Officer on the Lord Mayor's Day gave the fatal Wound to the Lady's Heart. *Oxford Journal, 26 November 1768*

1769

Mr. J. Hatton, hardware and toyman... eloped with Miss Duddy of Chatham [Kent], an agreeable young lady of genteel fortune, who were married at Ferne, about twelve miles from Dunkirk: they returned again immediately, and were re-married last Saturday at the Cathedral, with the consent of all parties.

Kentish Gazette, 25 February 1769

This letter, published in the Bath Chronicle and Weekly Gazette on 9 November 1769, may be an apocryphal tale concocted by journalists:

"A copy of a letter from the sister of a Right Hon. Lord, who lately eloped with a Gentleman to France, addressed to her Mother.

Calais, Oct. 25, 1769

Dear Madam

I have anticipated every paternal uneasiness you must have felt from the moment you discovered I had left you: as I have therefore been the occasion of it, I think myself in duty bound to give you as early an explanation of my conduct as possible, flattering myself, when you come to balance it properly in your mind, I shall be acquitted even from your understanding, without the interposition of maternal tenderness.

Ever since I could associate an idea, I have looked upon matrimony as the source from whence we were to draw the most finished happiness, or accumulated misery. Clear in this opinion, I thought persons could not be too circumspect in their choice, and that every thing that led to this, was to be primarily pursued. I was confirmed in this theory, by the contrary practice of most of my acquaintance, who dedicating their pursuits to interests and connections, so far lost sight of happiness, that divorces frequently succeeded the marriage-rites; however, shocked by such examples I was determined to benefit by the lesson. Mr. M— introduced himself to my acquaintance; his person, his manner, his address; in short, that quelque chose that determines every sentimental man or woman's fate in love, soon furthered the introduction to my heart. Our mutual sentiments thus known, the rest may be easily guessed; I agreed to marry and elope with him; a post-chaise and four soon carried us to Dover, and a few hours afterwards we landed here.

As my husband may want the fortuitous appendages of rank and fortune, I expect to be told I have acted imprudently and meanly; but this is a vulgar error, that, amongst many others, is adopted without any authority. How can I be guilty of the former when I have acquired every thing my heart wished for? or how of the latter, when by the laws of nature he is my equal.

Be superior then, my dear Madam, to vulgar opinions! consider how much better it is to see your daughter happy, than either rich or titled; pleased, tho' in a humble situation, than miserable, in an elevated one; the affectionate wife of Mr. M—, than the legal prostitute of some Right Hon. Lord.

I shall leave you with these reflections, hoping they will produce the wished for consequences, and beg leave to subscribe myself,

With great duty and respect,
Your affectionate daughter
*** ******"

A letter from Carlisle informs us, that an unknown gentleman, and a beautiful young lady, who had eloped from her friends in London, and been married at Edinburgh, returning from thence on horseback, were both unfortunately drowned as they were attempting to cross the river Eske, near Bonus.

Kentish Gazette, 12 December 1769

1770

Thursday, at Penrith races, Mr John Roddus, mason, of Graystock [Greystoke] Castle [near Penrith, Cumbria], and Miss Mally Hoggart, of Newbiggin [Northumberland], eloped from the race ground (whilst the horses were running a heat) on a matrimonial jaunt to Scotland, and were married at Gretna-Green before their plot was suspected. The young lady is very amiable and has a fortune of £1000. How fleet the wings of love.

Leeds Intelligencer, 29 May 1770

A young lady of distinction eloped one day last week from the neighbourhood of St James's church [London], with a tradesman in the city, who passed for near a month, among the young lady's friends, for the Son and heir of a distinguished Nobleman.

Leeds Intelligencer, 5 June 1770

Saturday last the Daughter of an eminent Merchant, near the Change [Royal Exchange, London], eloped with her Father's Footman, but being pursued they were overtaken at Dunstable [Bedfordshire], and the Lady obliged to return, to the great Disappointment of herself and Lover.

Northampton Mercury, 18 June 1770

A few days ago a Maiden Lady pretty advanced in years, eloped with a coachman, that had formerly lived with her father as a servant. What is remarkable, being both of age, they were married by licence at a neighbouring church, where the Lady was instantly known, and the news conveyed to her Father's house before the ceremony was well over; but it was wholly discredited, as Miss used to rail at such clandestine marriages, that entailed disgrace upon families, with a bitterness that every body thought was natural and would have defended her from a like indiscretion. *Reading Mercury, 25 June 1770*

A few days since a young lady, the only child of a gentleman in Berkley [sic] Square [London], eloped with her music master, and has not since been heard of; being a Dutchman, it is supposed he has taken her to Holland. *Leeds Intelligencer, 31 July 1770*

On Saturday last a young lady of fortune, in Spitalfields [east London], made an excursion to France in company with a French hair-dresser. *Leeds Intelligencer, 31 July 1770*

From Brighthelmstone [Brighton in Sussex] we hear, that last Sunday a very beautiful young lady, with a large fortune, eloped from her relations at that place; she jumped out of a one-pair-of-stairs [first floor] window into her gallant's arms.

Kentish Gazette, 21 August 1770

On Saturday the daughter of an eminent merchant near the 'Change, who lately had an independent fortune of fifteen thousand pounds, left her by an uncle, eloped with her father's clerk, and has not since been heard of.

Oxford Journal, 25 August 1770

The young gentleman who shot himself a few days ago in Vine Street [in the West End of London], was to have set off for Scotland the evening before with a young lady whom he had courted for some time, and had obtained the mother's consent; but on a sudden it was broke off by the interposition of an interested person: in consequence of which, the parties agreed to elope to Scotland and had prepared a chaise; but as the young lady, with her attendant, was stepping in, she fainted away and on coming to herself, declared she could not undertake the plan for fear it should give her mother too great uneasiness, and persuaded the lover to go back with her to the house, to urge further intreaties to consent; where, meeting with a rebuff, he went home to his own lodgings in Piccadilly, and was found dead with a pistol at his ear the next morning. *Oxford Journal, 20 October 1770*

A young Lady of Fortune lately eloped from her Father's House, near Tenbury in this County, with an Attorney's Clerk. It is thought they are set out for Scotland.

Oxford Journal, 8 December 1770

1771

The 25th ult. The celebrated Mrs. Ann Kanair, relict [widow] of David Kanair, of Berwick upon Tweed, made an elopement to Scotland, in a post-chaise, on a marrying jaunt, with Mr. McDonald; a gentleman well stricken in years, but possessed of an ample fortune. *Newcastle Courant, 9 March 1771*

A few days since the daughter of a publican in Westminster, eloped with a young fellow of that neighbourhood, and took with her notes and cash to the amount of one hundred and sixty pounds; her father suspecting intrigue, told her that if she went after such a fellow he would cut off her legs; the girl said he might if he pleased, but it would signify little, for she would follow him on the stumps. *Kentish Gazette, 24 August 1771*

Last Saturday a young lady, who lived with her aunt, not far from Lincoln's Inn Fields [London], being sent to Clare Market, attended by the footman, instead of going there made an elopement with him. She has a fortune in her own hands, left by an uncle. It is supposed they are gone to the North.

Leeds Intelligencer, 27 August 1771

A few days ago a young lady of fortune, in the forest of Dean, in Gloucestershire, eloped with a young fellow; and, to avoid the imputation of his stealing her, she rode first on the horse, and stole him. *Leeds Intelligencer, 24 September 1771*

The first escape of the young lady from the house of her nominal uncle at Woolwich was effected we are informed in the following manner:– The morning of the day of the elopement the uncle went to the young lady's aunt at Richmond [Surrey], in order to prevail on her to take charge of her. In his absence the young matross [soldier of artillery], with his friends, having consulted respecting what was to be done, that evening, at six o'clock, went to the old gentleman's house in the dock yard, and made a forcible entry. The young man who was to have been married to her, immediately locked the gates and then went to a neighbouring justice of the peace for assistance. In the interim the girl was taken out of the window, and when the gates were opened to admit the Justice, the matross made his way, with his sword in his hand, and the lady in the other, and effected their escape to London. The lady, it seems, is a natural daughter of the late

Lord A—, who left her a good fortune, and her mother was the wife of one of the surgeon's mates on board the Admiral's ship. She is now living, and a widow. The person at Woolwich, who is called her uncle at the request of Lord A—'s family, is not related to her.

The above young lady was brought back by her friends on the 14th instant. She has since, however, been again taken away by violence, by certain persons, under the pretence of an arrest, who broke open the lock of her chamber and parlour doors, and forced her out of the window. *Leeds Intelligencer, 5 November 1771*

A terrible *Fracas* happened very lately at K. N— [possibly, King's Nuympton], Devonshire. Miss Kitty B. (niece of the present Lord C.) and her Mamma's postilion, were discovered in *modo amoroso*, rehearsing *une Petite Piece de Theatre* [sic, theatrical act], called the Pleasures of the Stable, in the new Method as it is acted by Lady Ligonier, Mrs. Bailey, and others. The Parties have amused themselves this Way, it is said, with *the utmost pleasure*, for more than a Twelvemonth past. By the swain's letters (which may vie with 'Squire Morgan's for grammatical nicety and elegant diction) it appears that the Elopement, or a Trip to Scotland, was soon to be performed. *Northampton Mercury, 25 November 1771*

Penelope Ligonier, née Pitt in 1749, had a scandalous affair with the Italian poet and dramatist Count Vittorio Amadeo Alfieri.

1772

Wednesday night, at nine o'clock, Miss D. of St James's Square [London], eloped from her friends with Lieut. J.B. of Sackville-street, supposed to be gone for France.

Bath Chronicle and Weekly Gazette, 16 January 1772

FIG.26 Modern Love, Plate 2, the Elopement, engraved by John Goldar after John Collet (1765). A young woman has crossed a high paling into the arms of her lover, a dragoon. An old hag, holding a purse in her left hand, assists. A post-chaise, bearing the motto 'Ready', waits beyond the palings. At the foot of the ladder is a rectangular box tied with ribbon, inscribed 'For Miss Fanny Falsestep'. On the right is a noticeboard: 'Notice is hereby given that a Man Trap is set every Night within these Pales'. A signpost in the lane points (left) 'To London' and (right) 'This leads to the Great Northern Road'
The Colonial Williamsburg Foundation, 1969-100

Wednesday morning a linen-draper's daughter, not far from the Royal Exchange, thought proper to elope with her father's youngest apprentice, a youth about eighteen; the young lady is already entitled to £4000 by the death of an aunt.

Oxford Journal, 16 May 1772

A correspondent informs us, that the Lord Chancellor has already been consulted on the late elopement of a patriotick Secretary with the natural daughter of a late Lord, the young lady being very little more than twelve years of age...

The gentleman reported to have taken a trip with his ward, is said not to have gone to Scotland but to Flanders. We are told that in the former place the age of fourteen is the soonest they will suffer any parties to enter into the marriage state and this lady is not thirteen. *Oxford Journal, 30 May 1772*

In 1772 29-year-old barrister Robert Morris abducted his twelve-year-old ward Frances Mary Harford, the illegitimate daughter (and recent heiress to £30,000) of his deceased friend Lord Baltimore, from her Chelsea boarding-school. He fled with her to Europe and put her through two marriage ceremonies, at Ypres and in Danish Holstein. Multiple court cases over the next twelve years kept the newspaper-reading public appalled, thrilled and entertained. Eventually, in 1784, after complex legal wranglings, the marriage was annulled in the English ecclesiastical courts. Frances, now aged twenty-four, married William Frederick Wyndham a few months later. In 1791 Morris sailed for India, aiming to practise law there but was refused a licence. He died in Utah Pradesh at the age of fifty.

On Thursday evening a young lady, daughter of a gentleman in Great George Street, Westminster, eloped with her father's footman, and carried off notes to the amount of £1500 and yesterday her father cut his throat in so dangerous a manner, that his life is despaired of. *Ipswich Journal, 17 October 1772*

1773

Extract of a letter from Pembrokeshire, (Wales) dated Feb 1.

On Monday the 18th of January a three-masted vessel called the Phoebe and Peggy, was driven by stress of weather into Bride's Bay, near the Mouth of Solva, a sea port, within 4 miles of St David's, in this county. She rode there with one anchor, having lost two, with the cables. The captain's name was David M'Cullough. She was bound from Philadelphia to Newry, in Ireland, laden with linseed, staves, some puncheons of rum, and cocoa. The ship's crew and passengers were 64 in number, 5 of whom were women. The inhabitants of Solva immediately assembled to give them all the assistance they could; but the sea was so boisterous they durst not attempt it...

Several of the bodies have been found, particularly the five women, among whom was a wealthy merchant's daughter, who had eloped with her lover; she had remarkable fine long hair, and swam a great way, and was observed every now and then to throw the waves aside, and had she fortunately directed her course to the nearest shore, she might have saved her life. Her paramour, supposed to be either a Quaker or a Papist, would not suffer the Vicar of Whitchurch to read the funeral sermon over her, but read some prayers, said to be Latin, all the way to the churchyard, and at the interment. The young woman had in her pocket a small Bible and Common Prayer when left by the tide. *Derby Mercury, 26 February 1773*

The Phoebe and Peggy was lost in a severe gale on St Eves Rock in St Brides Bay on 19 January 1773. Four captains of Solva vessels went out in small boats and managed to board eighteen survivors but the boats were then smashed on the rocks, drowning twelve passengers, three crewmen and the four rescuers. Some sixty lives were lost in total. Some of the local population plundered the bodies of the drowned for jewellery, coins and clothes. The victims were later buried in Brawdy Church. The veracity of the Derby Mercury's story of the eloping couple is unverified.

The eldest son of a great family, a youth about 20, has eloped to Scotland with his mother's maid. *Newcastle Courant, 5 June 1773*

Saturday a genteel young fellow, Clerk to a wholesale dealer in Wood Street, absconded with a considerable sum of money he had been entrusted to receive, and was overtaken next morning in a post-chaise near St Alban's, with a young lady of fortune who had eloped from her guardians at Lowlayton [Leyton, Waltham Forest].

Oxford Journal, 20 November 1773

1775

Monday a young lady, who that day came of age, and has an independent fortune of five hundred a year, eloped from her father's house in Westminster, with his footman, and lay that night in a milk cellar in the neighbourhood of Covent Garden, the owner of which being the only friend the hero could introduce his bride to for a night's lodging. *Leeds Intelligencer, 25 April 1775*

Yesterday a beautiful young lady, and much admired for her smart wit and repartee, eloped from her parents, who live in a very splendid situation, not far from the Royal Exchange, with a servant who has lived in the family as valet-de-chambre for upwards of six years, and it is supposed they are gone to Scotland. The young lady took with her jewels, money and other valuables, to the amount of £1000, which were in her own possession, and she is intitled to a very considerable fortune in her own right next March or April.

Ipswich Journal, 7 October 1775

1776

Two days since a journeyman barber eloped with the daughter of a clergyman of this city [Ipswich], on a supposition, it is supposed, of her having £8000 but alas, the young lady has not a shilling in possession or dependence, but what is at the will of her parent. May not the barber really be said to be in the suds?

Ipswich Journal, 13 April 1776

Yesterday morning a young lady of fashion, in the neighbourhood of St. James's Park, made an elopement with her father's butler. It is said she has £20,000 at her own disposal.

Ipswich Journal, 15 June 1776

Saturday evening a young lady of Parliament-street, Westminster, who is, when of age, entitled to a genteel fortune, eloped with a black servant of her father's.

Ipswich Journal, 19 October 1776

The youngest daughter of a wealthy inhabitant of [London], eloped on Monday morning, about two o'clock, with her father's footman; and before ten o'clock seven different persons were dispatched after them. The lovers had been at the Lord Mayor's Ball on Saturday evening. *Oxford Journal, 16 November 1776*

A young maiden of spirit, the daughter of a cork-cutter in the city, to shew herself as close an imitation of ladies of fashion in her passions, as in the height of her headdress, eloped lately with her father's journeyman, upon a matrimonial expedition to Scotland. But to elope in the simple style of Corydon and Phillis [the subjects of a bawdy late seventeenth-century song about a shepherd and shepherdess], was ill-suited to the spirit and vivacity of the cork-cutter's daughter; and her strong attachment to her intended partner for life, let her wits to work to prevent any discovery or impediment to the completion of her wishes; she proposed therefore to her lover they should set off in the disguise of a sailor's habit. Accordingly two dresses were provided, the lovers were dressed, and set off on foot to the inn, where the post chaise was ready to receive them; but unfortunately a press-gang met them on the way, seizing the young tars, and it was in vain that Miss in trowsers [sic] proclaimed herself a female; away they were hurried to the regulating captain, who out of politeness to the fair sex, would not suffer the she-tar to accompany her lover, and some other captives on board the tender that night. The next morning to gratify the naval genius of his young tar, the captain carried her on board the tender to shew her the happiness of a sailor's life: there she found her unfortunate lover in the distress that might be expected for the loss of his mistress: but he began to revive at the sight of his dear Amelia [an allusion to Henry Fielding's sentimental novel of that name]: yet to prove that the sailor is as successful with the ladies as a soldier, the lover found no other relief than his deary's procuring his discharge from the captain, and desiring him to return her to her father and not blab.

Leeds Intelligencer, 26 November 1776

1777

On Monday last a young Lady, not far from Cavendish-square [London], eloped with a French Dancing-Master; she is said to have no less than £70,000 in her own Possession, and considerably more in Expectation after the death of an elderly Aunt. *Derby Mercury, 14 February 1777*

Wednesday a young lady, an orphan, entitled to a fortune of £17,000 when of age, on the day of marriage, eloped from her guardian near Berkley-square with a man of the Ton [a person of fashion], who was very lately a horse doctor to several gentlemen of the turf. *Ipswich Journal, 9 August 1777*

It is reported at the west end of town, that the daughter of a rich old knight has eloped with a Jew of the Temple (lately come from Italy): What is more remarkable is that the little Israelite has chosen a girl who is not dependant upon her parents, as the lady has £8000 left her not a year ago by an old maiden aunt.

Caledonian Mercury, 1 October 1777

1778

We hear from Sutton in Ashfield, near Mansfield [Nottinghamshire], that a very ludicrous and extraordinary Affair, and yet no stranger than true, happened last Week at that Place: Two men having for some Time past courted one Woman, and all three living in the same House, G—s and the Girl were asked in the Church, and accordingly Preparations were made for their Wedding on the 28th past; the Bridegroom, Bride-Maid and Father, repaired to the Church, the Minister waiting for them; but to their great Disappointment, the Girl was eloped with her other Suitor, who having procured a Licence, returned on the 29th in the Night, and rode to Swanwick to get her Parents Consent, the girl being under Age; but whilst he was talking with the father, G—s being in Bed at the same House, found means to get through a Window, and mounting the other Person's Horse, rode off undiscovered to the Girl at Sutton, whom he called out of Bed, and was married to her on the 30th past, whilst her other Suitor was seeking for his Horse.

Derby Mercury, 2 October 1778

On Saturday a young lady, the daughter of a capital merchant, eloped with her father's coachman; but the old gentleman, having intelligence of their route, set off in a post chaise and four, and overtook them at an inn near Coventry. What is remarkable, the young lady was by her father previously engaged in a matrimonial contract to a tradesman near the Change [Royal Exchange], with a portion of £15,000. The young lady has been brought back, but positively declares that she will never marry any person who is not the object of her own choice. She has an independent fortune lately left her by a relation of £700 per annum.

Ipswich Journal, 28 November 1778

1779

Last Saturday morning, the only daughter of a reputable farmer in Essex eloped with a footman in the neighbourhood, whom she married the same morning. Her conduct had so great an effect on her mother that she cut her throat in a shocking manner; whether she is dead or not, we have not yet heard. The above young lady had a portion of £4000 and at the death of her father perhaps would have received a fortune of £20,000 had she not disobliged him. By an advertisement in the London Evening Post, the above person appears to be Miss Ann Rivers, of Downham near Billaricay, a lady aged 17 years.

Ipswich Journal, 6 November 1779

1780

A young gentleman of the name of [John] Brisbane, who some time ago eloped from Bath, and married the daughter of Col. Martin, a gentleman of large fortune in the West of England, a few days ago took a draught of poison, at his lodgings in Winchester, and afterwards went in a post-chaise to the White Horse at Rumsey, where he died. It is said he pressed Mrs. Brisbane, who was with him, to take part of the dose, which, on her refusing, he drank himself.

Hampshire Chronicle, 23 October 1780

Capt. Brisbane, who deprived himself of life by poison not many days since, had eloped from Bath with a young lady of fortune, but not an independent one. The father, so far from being reconciled with his daughter or son-in-law, upbraided the latter with his having taken his daughter from him: and, it is reported, that he took no small pains to persuade his daughter to leave her husband, and put herself under the protection of her parent. This she peremptorily refused to do, and by her refusal, enraged her father greatly. After they had been married about two months, the husband was arrested, and carried to a sponging house [a place of temporary confinement for debtors], whither his lady accompanied him. The young gentleman was at length released, by means of a friend, endued with a feeling and truly amiable disposition; one, "who had a tear for pity, and a hand open as day for melting charity." The young couple were received into the house of their friend, where they met with a hearty welcome in every respect. Soon after their departure from this hospitable roof, the unfortunate event happened, which we may pity, though we can't approve. *Ipswich Journal, 4 November 1780*

John Brisbane was buried on 18 October 1780 at Romsey in Hampshire. A note on the register reads, 'poysoned himself at Winton & died at the White Horse'.

1781

A very singular and affecting Case is now depending in the Court of Chancery, which was in part argued on Friday last before the Chancellor of Lincoln's Inn Hall.

One of the Guardians of a young Lady, whose Name was [Catherine] Grierson, from Manchester, and lately at boarding School in Battersea, 16 Years old, and a Ward of the Court, brought on a Suit against a young Gentleman of the Name of Williamson [an error — his name was Thomas Thomasson], a Captain in the Navy, for marrying the young Lady at Gretna Green, in Scotland, and thereby incurring a Contempt, for which he was finally committed to the Fleet Prison: When the Sentence was passed, the young Lady (who was in Court, standing near her Husband, and whose Beauty and unaffected Modesty captivated the Eye at least of every Spectator) fainted away, and which she was with Difficulty recovered, when she immediately fell into strong Fits, in which Condition she was carried off; such an unusual Picture of Distress drew Tears

FIG.27 Thomas King and Sophia Baddely in *The Clandestine Marriage*, a comedy of manners first performed in 1766 and written by George Colman the Elder and David Garrick, by Richard Earlom aft. Johan Joseph Zoffany (1772). The plot concerns the daughters of a merchant, one of whom has secretly married a clerk.
Yale Center for British Art, Paul Mellon Collection. B1977.14.14614.

from every Eye: The Judge on the Bench was observed two or three Times to dry his Eyes. His Answer to the Enquiry was, "he knew not whether such Marriages were agreeable either to the Laws of Earth or Heaven;" and therefore referred it to the Master of Chancery for Enquiry.

On Friday Evening several of the most eminent Counsel waited on the Lord Chancellor at his House setting forth the lamentable Situation of the young Lady, whose Life is despaired of; who declared, that he wished most sincerely to relieve the distrest Couple, and if they would point out a Mode, in which it might be done consistent with the Duty of an equitable Judge, he would most willingly adopt the Measure.

The Consequence of this was, an Order on Saturday Morning that the Captain would be restricted to the Rules of the Fleet Prison, and that his Lady be with him, till a Messenger who is sent to Scotland, arrives with an Account of the reality of the Marriage.

Mrs. Williamson [Thomasson] continues to lie dangerously ill without Hopes of recovery.

Her Guardians are, by her Father's will, her Mother, a Friend, and an Uncle: One of the relations, who is the next Heir, in case of the Lady's decease before him, is the Apellant of this Business; the other two Guardians have shewn no Aversion to the Match, the young Officer's Character appearing to be irreproachable.

Derby Mercury, 2 August 1781

The petitioner [Mrs. Grierson] therefore hoped his lordship would upon the circumstances stated in the master's report, deem the marriage to be valid, and would discharge him out of custody, he submitting to execute any settlement the court might please to order; and therefore prayed it to be referred to the master to approve of a proper settlement to be made on Catherine Grierson, the infant, the petitioner agreeing to execute the same, or such other as might be approved of by the court, and in the mean time to discharge the prisoner Thomasson from his commitment, in order to effect a marriage according to the laws of this country.

After hearing counsel on behalf of the petitioners, his

lordship was pleased to order that Thomas Thomasson should be discharged from confinement, and said, if the practice of running away with wards continued, the court must punish more severely.

His lordship advised the mother to have the gentleman and lady again married, and he took occasion to observe, that it was a matter of doubt in his mind how far the crossing over from one side of a brook to the other, and immediately returning, legalised those Scotch nuptials. The re-union, however, of this happy pair gave great satisfaction to the persons present.

The Hibernian Magazine, December 1781

Catherine Grierson and Thomas Thomasson were married by banns at St. Bride's, Fleet Street in London, on 5 November 1781. There was one known child from the marriage, Catherine, born in 1784.

Aug. 26. At Gretna Green, Theophila, aged 38, widow of — Green, Esq; and one of the daughters of Mr. Wildman, salesman, London, [was married] to John Schreiber, son of Charles Schreiber, Esq; of Enfield, aged 17, heir to a fortune of £100,000.

The Scots Magazine, 1 September 1781

This Day a Petition was presented to the Lord Chancellor, in Lincoln's Inn Hall, by Mr. S[chreiber], stating, that his Son, a Ward of that Court, was an Infant, of Seventeen Years of Age, that he was sent for his Education, to a Village, within ten Miles of London, under the Tuition and Care of the Rev. Mr. Stevens, who was to have an Allowance of £250 per Annum, that on the third of March he was informed by Mr. Stevens that his Son had eloped about Eleven O'Clock the preceding Evening; he had since discovered that his Son had been decoyed away by several Persons, and influenced to marry Mrs. Green, a Widow, he therefore prayed for Judgement against Mrs. Green, her Mother, Mrs. Wildman, and a Relative, for a Contempt of that Court. A variety of Affidavits, stating the Manner in which the Transaction was performed, were read, and no Denial of the Facts being offered by the accused, the Lord Chancellor expatiated in the most animated and pathetic Terms upon the Infamy of trepanning Infants into improper and dishonourable Marriages, and he was much concerned that the Power of that Court extended no farther than to the Punishment of Offences so atrocious only by Imprisonment. In this Case, a Confederacy had been formed by the Persons before him, and others unknown, to seduce an Infant away, and marry him to a Person, who, whatever had been her previous character, was, by her consenting and abetting this Seduction, a very Improper Person to be connected with a respectable Family: He observed in the Affidavits, there was a Description of a Mrs. W. who had by her own Confession been an active Person in this infamous Transaction; he therefore ordered that she should attend, with the rest of the Parties on the next Day for hearing Petitions. He expressed himself pretty severely against the Tutor as having very probably been, in some Measure, one of the Confederates, although there is no direct Evidence of his Guilt; but it was exceeding suspicious, that he should be apprized of the Elopement at Seven O'Clock in the Morning, and yet did not acquaint his Father with it until Five o'Clock in the Afternoon.

With regard to the Infant, he ordered him to be returned to his Father, and recommended proceeding against the Delinquents in the court of King's Bench, which Court would no doubt upon conviction inflict a more exemplary Punishment than it was competent in him to do.

The Infant, as he was legally termed, led his Wife to an elegant Carriage which stood in the Yard, with the greatest Gallantry and Care; she was so overcome by Heat arising from the great Crowd, that she was with much Difficulty prevented from fainting.

It is a little remarkable that Mrs. Green has £300 per Annum annuity, and £2000 in the Funds, is a Woman of exceedingly good Character, and irreproachable Morals, and was very much respected by a numerous and genteel Acquaintance.

Derby Mercury, 1 November 1781

John Schreiber and Theophila Green were remarried by banns on 22 October 1781 at St. Giles without Cripplegate in London. Theophila gave her name as 'Temperance'.

FIG.28 A Worn Out Debauchée, by Thomas Rowlandson (between 1790 and 1795). The newspaper-reading public was simultaneously fascinated and outraged by age differences in eloping couples. *Yale Center for British Art, Paul Mellon Collection. B1975.3.100*

1782

On Saturday morning last the Negro Servant of a Gentleman in the Neighbourhood of Mary[le]bone ran off with his Master's Niece, a fine young Lady about Seventeen. As soon as the Elopement was known, several persons were dispatched in pursuit of them. The Lady will be worth £11,000 when of age.

Oxford Journal, 2 March 1782

On Saturday last passed thro' Ferrybridge, on a matrimonial trip to Gretna-Green, [John Fane] the Right Hon. the Earl of Westmorland, with Miss [Sarah Ann] Child, daughter of Robert Child, Esq; banker in London; a young lady about 18 years of age, whose fortune will undoubtedly be upwards of half a million. *Leeds Intelligencer, Tuesday 21 May 1782*

Extract of a letter from Aikenbury-hill, in Huntingdonshire.
Friday morning, ten o'clock.

"I left London last night at ten o'clock on business, in to Nottinghamshire, and am got thus far in my road. We have had the strangest rout and pursuit upon the road all night that I ever heard of. The parties are the Earl of Westmorland running away with Miss Child the Banker's daughter...

"The pursuers are Miss Child's father, and another gentleman, in a post-chaise and four, and two servants. The gentlemen in the chaise are about two hours behind the fugitives; but the two servants came up with and endeavoured to pass Lord Westmorland, and his people (in order to buy up the chaises) about two miles, on the other side of Baldock [Hertfordshire], from London.

"Lord Westmorland's people suspecting their intention, stopped the two servants, and a severe conflict ensured:– they pulled Child's men off their horses, and fired their pistols into the bowels of one of the horses, which killed him on the spot. Being about to use the other horse in the same way, Child's people consented to stop, and quit the pursuit. The other horse lies dying with fatigue.

"All the horses at Newark were also taken, so that no probability remains of any interruption to the match. What Mr. Child's motives could be in objecting to a connection with a man of Lord Westmorland's excellent character is not very intelligible, but there is at present every reason to believe, that his Lordship will succeed in taking what the old gentleman so absurdly refused to give."

In confirmation of the above, Mr. Child was stopped at Newark, and Lord Westmorland, without interruption, succeeded in his marriage at Gretna Green, and is returned to London. Miss Child is about 18 years of age, whose fortune will undoubtedly be upwards of half a million. The Earl gave each postilion a guinea, and hostler 10*s* 6*d* [10 shillings and sixpence].

Newcastle Courant, Saturday 25 May 1782

Sarah Child's parents cut her out of their will, leaving their fortune to her second son or eldest daughter, in order that the Fane heir (and by extension the Fane family) did not gain.

1783

On Sunday se'evennight, the waiter of the Cock Inn, in Stony Stratford, Buckinghamshire, eloped with his mistress's daughter for Gretna Green, but was unfortunately overtaken at the Anchor in Loughborough, by two gentlemen of the short whip, who... returned with the lady in triumph, leaving the poor bilk't waiter to bemoan his hard fate. What is more extraordinary, this is the second time she has been overtaken in a similar excursion.

Leeds Intelligencer, 7 October 1783

Monday Miss C—— eloped from her friends in the city, but being missed in a few minutes by her parents, a pursuit was immediately made, and she was found at the door of a young lawyer in Chancery-lane, before he had time to open it. It is supposed their intention was for Gretna Green.

Morning Herald and Daily Advertiser, 10 September 1783

1784

An elopement has lately taken place in the fashionable world, which is now the subject of general conversation. One of the beautiful Miss Keppels [sic], daughter of the late bishop, has flown on the wings of love to the land of liberty, with the Hon Mr. [George Ferdinant] Fitzroy, son of Lord Southampton, and one of the officers in the Prince of Wales's household. The reason of the elopement is, that their friends did not consent to their nuptials. *Ipswich Journal, 3 July 1784*

Mrs. Keppel being so soon reconciled to the marriage of her second daughter Miss Laura Keppel to Capt. Fitzroy is entirely owing to the friendly part taken by the Prince of Wales. When it was made known to Mrs. Keppel, that her daughter had eloped, after the first effort of her concern had subsided, she sat down and wrote a very affecting letter to his Royal Highness complaining of the loss of her Laura, and requesting his assistance to recover her. The Prince, who, though a stranger to the elopement, was acquainted with the attachment that subsisted between the parties, immediately waited upon Mrs. Keppel, and about half hour's conversation prevailed with her to be reconciled to the young couple. His Royal Highness on his return to Carleton-House dispatched an express after the fugitives, and on their arrival in town accompanied them to Mrs. Keppel's, [from] where they were married. *Norfolk Chronicle, 20 July 1784*

Laura Keppel married George Ferdinand FitzRoy on 2 July 1784, when she was nineteen and he was twenty-three. George's father, Lord Southampton, had not been consulted about the match, but accepted it later. They went on to have two daughters. Laura became Lady of the Bedchamber to the Prince of Wales's hated wife Caroline of Brunswick.

Two runaway matches in the same family in the course of a few days, are events that seldom occur. The circumstances that have attended the life of our gallant Rodney, are not more singular than those of the younger branches of his house. His second son has long been enslaved by the personal and mental charms of Lady [Catherine] Francis [sic] Nugent, a daughter of the facetious Earl. Young [John] Rodney, though he had the good fortune to succeed in obtaining the favourable opinion of the Lady, could not possibly make any impression upon the mind of her father. Thus circumstanced, he was determined, if he could obtain the Lady's consent, to visit the borders of Scotland. Little persuasion was necessary to induce her to follow the bent of her inclination, and to Scotland they went, and had that knot tied which we trust nothing but death will separate. While these lovers were in pursuit of the completion of their wishes, the second daughter [Jane] of Lord Rodney, was prevailed on to follow the example of her brother, and in a few days after set out upon the same journey, stimulated by the same motives, with Captain [George] Chambers of the guards, son to Sir William Chambers, the celebrated architect. They had not proceeded far before they met Mr. Rodney and his Lady returning to town from Gretna Green. The meeting disconcerted both parties not a little; but an explanation instantly taking place, the brother declared he would not attempt to interrupt their journey, convinced that Captain Chambers had a sincere affection for his sister, and that a reconciliation with his father would soon take place. What adds to the singularity of the affair is, that the same post that brought Lord Rodney an account of the marriage of his son with Lady Frances Nugent, likewise brought him intelligence of his daughter's elopement. *Kentish Gazette, 4 September 1784*

Catherine Frances Nugent was the daughter of Thomas Nugent, Earl of Westmeath; John Rodney was the son of Admiral George Brydges Rodney, 1st Baron Rodney. Both were under age when they married some time before July 1784, when they repeated the ceremony at St. Marylebone Church, London. Catherine died in 1794. John, a naval captain, went on to marry twice more, and died in 1847. George Chambers and Jane Rodney, eighteen and seventeen, married by licence 12 September 1784 at Croft in North Yorkshire.

1785

Fanny Fust was the only surviving child of Denton Fust of Clifton, Bristol, whose family was long established in Gloucestershire. She had inherited not only her father's fortune but also, through her uncle, the vast and lucrative Hill Court estate. In the language of the time, she had an 'imbecility of mind' and this made her especially vulnerable to predatory suitors. In 1785, Henry Pawlet Bowerman, about whom little is known, made Fanny, now twenty-one, his target, showering her with attention.

On Wednesday Mr. Mingay moved the court of King's Bench, for a rule to shew cause why an information should not be filed, by the master of the Crown Office, against Henry Pawlet Bowerman, esq, his brother John Bowerman, Matthew Willick, esq., and his wife and the two Miss Paynes, for conspiring to carry off Miss [Fanny] Fust...

This young lady, just turned of 21, appears to be the niece of Sir John Fust, upon whose death she becomes entitled to an estate of £2000 per annum, and is also possessed of a very considerable fortune derived from the death of her father. From her infancy, however, she has labored under so unfortunate an imbecility of mind, that it was necessary a confidential servant should be placed over her, to superintend, and in a great measure to direct her actions.

Upon this rich prize H.P. Bowerman had for some time meditated an essay of gallantry and had, in some measure, found opportunities of breathing love-tales into her unsuspecting ear; but the jealous eyes by which she was hourly watched, obstructed their frequency, and prevented the courtship from rising to its full maturity. Despairing, therefore, of enjoying the rich harvest of his assiduities by the regular and gradual approach of the lover, he determined by one vigorous effort of dauntless gallantry to carry her off. For this purpose, Mr Bowerman made himself agreeable in the family of Mrs. Payne, who was upon terms of familiar intimacy with the mother and aunt of the rich heiress; and the Miss Paynes,

FIG.29 Marriage à la mode, Plate 1 'The Contract', engraving by Gerard Jean Baptiste Scotin after William Hogarth (1745). The first of a series of six plates illustrating the perils of marrying for money rather than love and satirising the morals of the upper classes.
Yale Center for British Art, Paul Mellon Collection, B2019.24.44

with a disposition natural to the young and lively of the sex, were soon induced to listen to the scheme.

Soon after the three ladies arrived at Mrs. Payne's Mr. Bowerman made his appearance; and shortly after that a post-chaise and four horses drove up to the door. It did not appear whether during the short interval which followed, Miss Fust was prevailed upon to accompany her hero, or whether she reluctantly entered the chaise; but Mr Bowerman, by some means, drove furiously away with the lady.

The lady's family, alarmed at the length of her visit, sent an escort to fetch her home. The elopement was thus discovered; alarm took place, enquiries were made, scouts were instantly dispatched round the country, but no tidings could be obtained. Soon afterwards, however, certain intelligence was received of their being on the road to France.

One of the judges of the King's Bench, on being applied to granted a *habeas corpus*, but before the officer had got half his journey, to execute the writ, Mr. Bowerman, his brother, one of the Miss Paynes, and the lady eloping, were landed, as they thought, with security, upon the French shore; these endeavours to recover the person of Miss Fust from the possession of her paramour proving abortive, new measures for the purpose were immediately and vigorously adopted.

Mr. Lewis, the law agent employed for the family of the Fusts, procured letters to the duke of Dorset, the English ambassador at Versailles, stating the particulars of the transaction, and requesting his immediate interposition. His industry, assisted by the representations of the duke of Dorset, procured an edict from the French king, to seize the young lady in any part of his dominions. They were found at Lisle [in the Dordogne]; but Bowerman resisted the order of the king, claimed possession of the lady, as his true and lawful wife, and solemnly declared that they had been deliberately married at Tournay [Tournai]; Mr. Lewis's clerk immediately went to Tournay to enquire into the truth of Mr. Bowerman's story; and he there learnt that the monks of every convent in the place had been very seriously applied to by the parties to perform the holy office, but that they had *una voce* [with one voice] refused it. In consequence of this intelligence, the young gentleman returned to Lisle, executed the orders of the king, and restored Miss Fust to the custody of her family. The court without hearing more particulars granted a rule against the defendants, to shew cause why they should not be tried upon an information for this offence. *Chelmsford Chronicle, 16 November 1787*

A protracted court case ensued. Bowerman failed in his attempt to overturn the Lord Chancellor's decision to declare Fanny incompetent to decide to marry and to place her fortune in the hands of a committee, and the marriage was annulled. Fanny returned to Bristol and later lived at Hill Court, where, after her mother's death, she was cared for by her cousin Flora Langley, who inherited Fanny's fortune.

1786

A few days since a Kentish heiress eloped from her father's house at midnight with a marine, accompanied by a confidential friend, and were married at St. Clement's church. On the next day the bride and bridegroom were surprised at seeing their father's carriage stop at their door, and much more surprised to hear him address them in words like the following:– "My children, I am not come to storm or upbraid; I opposed your union from no selfish motives; my daughter's happiness was all I had in view; and as I once thought I could not better promote it, than by refusing my consent to your marriage, so I am now convinced that I could not more effectually destroy it, than by continuing my resentment. You must, therefore, both return with me, and my fortune shall be yours, and I trust my son-in-law, by his future conduct, will convince me, that he had more love for my daughter than my land." The hired lodgings were instantly discharged, and the young couple returned to their father's seat with more joy, if possible, than they left it.

Norfolk Chronicle, 4 February 1786

Probably an apocryphal story. *See page 137.*

1787

A Correspondent, upon whose Intelligence we may depend, has informed us, that the following extraordinary and melancholy Accident happened within these few Days at Liverpool.

An Officer had formed a very warm Attachment to a young Lady of the Place, and, with her Consent, had made Proposals to her Friends, which were not accepted. The Lover however still persevered, and finally prevailed on the young Lady to elope with him. The Evening was fixed, and Circumstances arranged. She was to escape from the Window of her Bed-Chamber, for which Purpose a Ladder was provided. The Lady was so exceedingly timid, that she would not consent to descend but on her Lover's Shoulders. He expostulated and represented the Danger, but in vain. He at length took her on his Back, but unfortunately, before they were Half Way down the Ladder, their Weight broke it, and they both fell into the Street. The Lady escaped with very little injury. The Gentleman broke both his Legs and one of his Arms. We are happy to hear that he is likely to recover. – *General Evening.* *Northampton Mercury, 17 November 1787*

1788

A pleasant elopement took place an evening or two ago. Lady A.M. [Anna Maria] Bowes, the daughter of Lady Strathmore, set off for the continent with Mr. Jessop, of the Society of the Inner-Temple, a young gentleman of promising talents. Lady A.M. Bowes's fortune was originally £20,000 and if it has been managed with care, must be now considerably increased. Her ladyship is in her seventeenth year. The lovers were vis a-vis [sic] neighbours, in Fludyer Street, by which they found means to hold frequent conferences, and from which they made a safe retreat.

Newcastle Courier, 24 January 1788

Sunday morning, very early, Lady Anna Maria Bowes, eldest daughter of Lady Strathmore, eloped from the house of Mrs. Parish, where she lived, in Fludyer-street, Westminster, with Mr.

Jessop, who had a house so contiguous, that the party contrived to lay boards from one to another; by the help of which, and a ladder, they had the pleasure of marching off without being discovered even by the watch, and are, by this time, on their way to Calais, the gentle God fanning a propitious gale! It appears that a correspondence has been carried on for near a twelvemonth past, by means of the servants in each family, yet not the least suspicion was ever entertained by Mrs. Parish. The gentleman is the son of a Col. Jessop, an American loyalist, and is a student in the Temple; the property of the family shared the fate of the rest of that unfortunate body in America. The lady is a ward in Chancery, is aged eighteen, and will possess a fortune of thirteen thousand pounds, when she comes of age. The chancellor will be applied to for the future protection of his ward.

Chelmsford Chronicle, 1 February 1788

The marriage between Anna Maria Bowes and Henry James Jessop was an unhappy failure. Anna's debt-ridden husband died young and left her a widow with two small daughters.

On Wednesday afternoon, the THREE beautiful daughters of Lady A——, well known in the annals of portrait painting, took French leave of their mother's house, escorted by THREE Gentlemen. The parties are supposed to have taken the high road to matrimony.

The Times, 29 February 1788

The unwarrantable liberty which has recently been taken with three amiable young Ladies, in certain morning prints of *illegitimate* fashion, demands the severest reprehension. The elopement with all its supposed circumstances, were gross falsehoods, fabricated by a well known combination of *Beings* who affect to record the events of high life, without having the *entre* of one private house of fashionable distinction.

The circumstance which furnished employment for the inventive faculty of the intelligent writers in question was simply this: Having reason to be dissatisfied with their situation at Lady

Archer's, the amiable sisters determined to change their place of residence; and with her privity – if not approbation, availed themselves of the hospitality of their relations, Lady Plymouth and Lady Catherine Long, who offered them an asylum, and at whose houses they now reside.

The Times, 3 March 1788

Miss Elizabeth Courtney [Courtenay], daughter of Lord Courtney, eloped on Thursday se'nnight from her father's house, Grosvenor-square, to Gretna Green, with the second son of the Duke of Beaufort. The particulars are these: The young runaway, the better to conceal her designs, had bespoken a fine new dress for the Duke of York's ball on the Friday evening. On the night preceding, Miss Courtney, being engaged with the family at a route [evening party], affected indisposition, and consequently remained at home. About twelve o'clock at night, she and her maid sallied forth, armed only with the quivers of Cupid. At the end of Duke-street a post-chaise was in waiting with the hero in it, and off the two lovers drove. The maid returned and went to bed. Being rather late in stirring in the morning, she was called by some of her fellow-servants. She then declared, that so far from over-sleeping herself, she really had not slept a moment, for that she knew she would be turned off in the course of the day. Then she candidly explained. The hue and cry was raised, but all in vain. Miss Courtney is a lady of a very reserved, modest and amiable disposition. The affection has lasted for some time. It was not from dislike to the match that Lord Courtney was angry at his daughter's elopement; on the contrary, he approved of it. But his Lordship's pride was hurt on discovering some time ago the mutual affection of the young pair to the Duke of Beaufort, who disapproved of it. His Lordship, highly piqued at his daughter having been rejected, he and his family endeavoured to ween the predilection of the young lady, but all in vain.

Ipswich Journal, 31 May 1788

Elizabeth Courtenay, aged twenty-one, and Lord Charles Henry Somerset, twenty, were married with parental consent at Hillingdon, Middlesex on 8 June 1788. They went on to have at least six children. Somerset became governor of the Cape of Good Hope. Elizabeth died in 1815, Somerset six years later.

On Thursday last Miss B—b—a M— went off with one of her father's grooms from their country residence in Kent, for Dover, on their way to France. She is a most beautiful young lady about seventeen, and when of age will enjoy an estate of four thousand a year, left to her by her aunt, the late Dowager G—. Her mother's maid, who is sister to the groom, was a principal agent in this business, and had got a suit of boy's clothes made up for Miss, in which she was equipped for her love expedition. The greatest precaution was taken to avoid a pursuit, and as the mansion lies a good way from any village, the groom contrived the night before the morning of his departure, to secrete all the bridles and saddles, and to give the horses he left at home a strong dose of physic each, so that if the saddles were found, the cattle should not be able to proceed far. At about four in the morning Miss being habited, sallied forth, and was conveyed on horseback as far as Foot's Cray, where a post chaise being hired, they flew towards Dover. The demon of envy, however, in the form of one of the footmen, who had a similar design on his master's daughter, having suspected the groom, he kept a close watch and discovered the flight to the parents, almost as soon as it was effected. Orders for pursuit were instantly issued, but there was neither saddle nor bridle to be found for a long time, and when found, the horses were incapable of duty, and thought to be poisoned. Some, however, were procured from a neighbouring peer, and our lovers so closely pursued (for the man at Foot's Cray knew the lady) that they were overtaken at Sittingbourne, and Miss snatched from the arms of her lover just as he was handing her into a chaise where they had changed horses. She was immediately conveyed home, where she is now closely confined, and her love gone God knows where. The opportunities which the groom had with Miss, in teaching her how to ride, of which exercise she grew amazingly fond, were many, and as he was deemed a favourite with his master, the young lady was often entrusted to his care without the presence of a third person. This should operate as a warning to the fashionable world, not to permit their daughters ever to ride out, unless some proper person accompanies them, for there are dangerous moments, when love grows too powerful for reason, and the natural weakness of the female sex not unwillingly concedes the athletic superiority of man. *The Times, 14 October 1788*

Miss Eliz. F——ge, has lately eloped with a Capt. Bland. The captain, before he took Miss off, sent all the family to sleep, with a dose of laudanum, which had such an effect on the coachman, who drank plentifully of the punch, that he is dangerously ill. Miss F——ge has been, without interruption, buckled to her love by the Gretna Green blacksmith, and will possess, when of age, £8000 a year in Northamptonshire. She was to have been married on the day of the morning on which she went off, to the brother of a noble Earl – and every thing but signing the settlement, and repeating the ceremony, was finished. The captain, however, had the consummation so devoutly wished by the Honourable bridegroom, and is now in possession of the Treasure at Dublin, where he means to reside until Miss's age counts three times seven. *Hampshire Chronicle, 27 October 1788*

1789

Louisa Hornby, the youngest daughter of the Governor [William Hornby, the Governor of Bombay, 1771–1784], has eloped with Mr. [George] Little, an Irish Gentleman, only nineteen [Louisa was nineteen, George was twenty-two]. They passed through Barnet, on their way to Scotland.

The young Lady found some difficulty to get off, the lover having been waiting in a chaise, from ten o'clock to three in the morning. Such a prize could not be a matter of trifling anxiety, as the Gentleman, though of a respectable family, had no fortune of his own.

Old Mr. Hornby says, that, as the young couple took French

leave of him, he shall do the same by them. It is, however, to be hoped that the parties will be reconciled.

Mr [John] Hunter, the East India Director [William Hornby's stepfather-in-law], and young Hornby, are gone towards Scotland, to meet the new-married couple on their return.

The Times, 29 July 1789

The marriage produced four sons, three of whom survived into adulthood.

A trip to Gretna Green. On Monday last Miss P—, of T—ll, in Yorkshire, a young lady of exquisite beauty and sensibility, with a fortune of thirty thousand pounds, eloped to Gretna Green with Mr C—, linen-draper, of D—, in the same county, a gentleman, allowed by all statuaries, who have had the pleasure of seeing him, to be the best-proportioned and finest figure of a man in the kingdom, being upwards of six feet high, and of the exactest symmetry.

There is a very remarkable circumstance attending the marriage:

Mr C— was to have been united to Miss G—, of Wakefield, and Miss P— to Mr G—, brother to Miss G—, the same day being appointed for both weddings; but, what a melancholy to relate, Mr and Miss G— died a few days previous to the time fixed for the solemnization. It was at the funeral of their respective lovers that this present couple first met; there being a familiarity in their cases, a sympathizing attachment immediately took place, and they were married within a month.

Caledonian Mercury, 21 December 1789

1790

The matrimonial elopement on the Continent between Miss Campbell and Mr. Jennings, has ended in a style the most unexpected:— they were pursued, it is said, by the father and mother of the young lady, and overtaken at Ostend; when the parents agreed to their being married, but having re-conducted the young lady into Picardy, they instantly withdrew their consent, and have commenced a prosecution against the lover.

Derby Mercury, 7 January 1790

Extract of a Letter from Chatham, Jan. 15.

"Last week a young gentleman from London, aged 18, eloped with a young lady, aged 16, the youngest daughter of Captain Ogilvie, (a half-pay officer of marines here) on a matrimonial excursion to Flanders, in the Emperor's (at least the Patriots) district, where they were married. They returned to this place on Monday last. The gentleman has no fortune at present in his possession, but has a dependance upon the death of his mother; and the lady has not the least expectation."

Kentish Gazette, 19 January 1790

1791

An elopement has taken place in the neighbourhood of Grosvenor-square. John, as he attended his young mistress last Monday, in a morning promenade, persuaded her to accompany him to Scotland, to be there hammered into wedlock on the reverend anvil of the coupling blacksmith of Gretna Green. The lady went off about one o'clock at noon, and her pursuers followed about seven in the afternoon. She is only twelve years of age, and the valet is above thirty. This is the consequence of trusting fashionable children to the care of fashionable footmen; and nothing can be more dangerous than to suffer youth of either sex, to keep up a familiarity with servants, and persons of vulgar, corrupted and dissipated manners.

Derby Mercury, 24 February 1791

On Sunday arrived at the India Arms in Gosport a young lady and gentleman from Havre-de-Grace [Maryland, United States of America]. They had not been long there before two gentlemen arrived, who appear to be the guardians of the lady, and who said she had eloped. They locked her up in a room by herself, but the young gentleman contrived means to take her off before the guardians' faces the same evening. He hired all the boats on the beach at Gosport and crossed the water to Portsmouth, where a post-chaise was waiting as a further conveyance. *Oxford Journal, 26 March 1791*

A few days since a Welsh heiress eloped from her father's house with a young officer, accompanied by a confidential friend, and were married. On their return home, the bride and bridegroom were much surprised to hear the father address them in words like the following: "My children, I am not come to storm or upbraid; I opposed your union with no selfish motives. My daughter's happiness was all I had in view, and as I once thought I could not better promote it than by refusing my consent to your marriage, so I am convinced that I could not more effectually destroy it by continuing my resentment. You must therefore both return with me, and my fortune shall be yours; and I trust, my son-in-law, by his future conduct, will convince me, that he had more love for my daughter than my land." *Norfolk Chronicle, 17 September 1791*

An almost exact duplicate of a story that appeared in the Norfolk Chronicle, 14 February 1786, in which the heiress was from Kent.

1792

On Sunday an elopement took place from a Boarding-school in Hackney [to the east of London]. The parties were a young lady of seventeen, who, on coming of age, will be entitled to a considerable fortune, and a Naval Officer of subaltern rank. They are supposed to have directed their course to Scotland — and before notice could be given to the friends of the young lady, were probably beyond the reach of pursuit.

Oxford Journal, 7 January 1792

Miss M—, the sister of Lady G— resided [in Beverley, Yorkshire] with her aunt, Mrs. H—. It was on Friday se'nnight that Mr. B— an American gentleman, who had lodged some time in the town, and had rendered himself acceptable to Miss—, called on this lady, and, while her aunt was in the second floor, persuaded her to step from the parlour with him into a post-chaise. No pursuit was attempted, and the couple arrived at Gretna Green in safety, from whence they have returned man and wife. On Sunday last, the bans for their second marriage were published in Beverley church. Miss M— is in her seventeenth year, and has accomplishments of mind and person, which might have rendered her valuable, had her fortune been less than it is. But she is the coheiress with Lady G— to the property of their father, the late attorney, and has probably not less than fifty thousand pounds... Mr. B— is a Gentleman of respectable character, between thirty and forty years of age. *Public Advertiser, 18 April 1792*

Mary Midgeley, seventeen, the sister of Lady Grantley, eloped with 32-year-old William Beverley. A daughter was born in 1796. Mary died in 1802 and William in 1823.

Mr. B—l, an Irishman, eloped last Thursday night, with Miss W—h, a young lady of large fortune, from the house of her parents, in the neighbourhood of St. James's [London]. They had only got as far as the eight mile stone on the Gretna Green road, when two footpads stopped them, and demanded their money. Mr. B. knew that cash was at that time of the utmost consequence to him, swore he would give them nothing, and desired the post-boys to drive on. Upon which one of the ruffians held the horses; the other dragged the Captain out of the chaise, exercised his cutlass upon him in a most inhuman manner; and then rifling his pockets of three twenty-pound notes, and nine guineas [£9 9*s*], made off. The poor girl fainted away; and the post-boys, in this emergency, put the wounded man into the chaise, and drove to the apothecary's in Barnet. The doctor was soon roused from his sleep, and after dressing the wounds (which are by no means of a dangerous nature) at the young lady's particular request, accompanied her home again. *Oxford Journal, 27 October 1792*

A REWARD of ONE HUNDRED GUINEAS, and a CAUTION to the CLERGY. Whereas MARY SEVERNE, an infant, just turned of 16 Years of Age, was taken away from Portman-square [London], where she was walking with her Governess, on Friday the 12th of October last, by JOSEPH STINTON, a Servant of her Father's, with an Intention, it is supposed, of being married to her; Whoever will apprehend the said Mary Severne, or give Information to her said Father, JOSEPH SEVERNE, of Munderfield House, near Bromyard, in the County of Hereford, Esq. or to Messrs. Shepheard and Williams of Boswell-court, near Lincoln's-inn, London, so that she may be apprehended, and safely delivered to her Parents before her Marriage according to the Rites of the Church of England, shall receive the above Reward, and be otherwise fully indemnified.

The said MARY SEVERNE is tall and lusty of her Age, and rather stoops; she has Freckles on her Face, very good Hair, rather inclining to be Red; had on when taken away, a green Riding Habit, brown Great Coat, and black Riding Hat. The said JOSEPH STINTON is about 28 Years of Age, upright in his Person, about five Feet eight Inches high, and has dark Hair, curled round; had on when he went away, a round Hat bound, brown Great Coat, with Buttons of the same Colour, blue Under Coat, also with Buttons of the same Colour, a black and white striped Waistcoat, Leather Breeches and Boots... *The Times, 3 November 1792*

...Miss is described as tall and lusty of her age, but rather stoops. Indeed, we think when a young lady runs away with her footman, she stoops a little too much!

Bath Chronicle and Weekly Gazette, 8 November 1792

Joseph Severne's offer of a reward was published in The Times and in regional newspapers and repeated on 8 and 19 November but it was already too late. Mary Severne and Joseph Stinton married on 4 November 1792 at St. Mary, Putney. The couple previously published banns at St. Botolph, Aldersgate, where a note in the parish register reads: 'The woman under age & against the father's consent'.

FIG.30 The Lover's Letter Box, by George Baxter. Date unknown. Secret communication with a lover was an element of the elopement trope. *Yale Center for British Art, Paul Mellon Collection. B1977.14.10626*

On Sunday the 11th inst. was married at Gretna Green, Mr. Richard Harrison, of the royal artillery, to Miss Goodfellow, of Cross Hill in Cumberland. The following singular circumstances attended this union:— William James, a bombardier of the royal artillery, paid his addresses to his young lady, who is under age, and an heiress. Having obtained her consent, he engaged Mr. Harrison, his friend, to accompany them to Gretna, that he might assist, in case of a rescue being attempted. He placed his intended bride upon a horse behind the last mentioned, and, mounting another himself, they set off for the temple of Hymen. Upon the road, they fell in with some company, to whom James could not restrain communicating his successful negotiation with the lady, and the prospect of his approaching happiness. In the mean time the lady, being, as appears, more anxious for the completion of her wishes, urged her conductor to a more speedy flight, and they alighted at Longtown, some time before the intended bridegroom. On his arrival, he found them taking a little refreshment, and, as ill luck would have it, he could not avoid reproaching them for "leaving him on the road." The lady retorted, pretty warmly, his want of attention; the friend of both interfered, and, in short, a violent quarrel ensued; blows were exchanged, and it required the salutary aid of the constable to restore quiet. When the parties had time to recollect themselves, the lady declared, that, from the specimen she had seen of Mr. James's gallantry, she was determined not to marry him, but, being at the same time resolved not to return home without a husband, she made a surrender of her person and two estates to Mr. Harrison, if he thought proper to accompany her to the place of their first destination. Mr. H. was too much a man of spirit to refuse the challenge; they were instantly upon horseback again, and the *Old Cobler* [sic] at Gretna soon made them one — and within a very few hours of their first acquaintance.

Hampshire Chronicle, 3 December 1792

Within these few days, a young daring son of Neptune bore away from her disconsolate friends, at Kingston, Miss W——, a maiden lady of sixty-eight! Miss was determined on an excursion to

Gretna Green; but, e'er they had reached Dunstable, fatigue and anxious expectation had so far overcome her, that she consented a Bedfordshire parson should bind them in the silken bands of Hymen. The lady possessed an estate of £1800 per ann. and about £60,000 in the funds. *Hampshire Chronicle, 3 December 1792*

1793

A young lady [who] eloped on Friday last with her French teacher... is but in her fifteenth year, & is the only daughter of a physician in Holborn, who is one of the people called Quakers. The young lady's wearing apparel was by the assistance of a maid servant removed from the house piecemeal, for some days previous, to the Frenchman's lodgings, and as he was not burthened with cash, the lady thought that a few articles of plate might be useful.

Every thing being thus prepared, on Friday morning the young lady left her father's house, and was received by her enamoured *Teacher*, who procured a hackney coach, put their boxes into it, and drove to a house adjoining the river at Rotherhithe off which lay a vessel bound to Ostend, to sail that evening. In this vessel they were to take their passage, but a *confidential friend* of the lady's went to the father, and communicated the whole of the circumstance to him; he immediately went to the office in Bow-street, where, on application to Mr. Justice Bond, he obtained the assistance of two of his officers to apprehend the fugitives by whom they were traced to the house in Rotherhithe, and taken, together with their boxes; they were conveyed before Mr. Bond, and late on Friday night, underwent an examination, when it appearing that the plate was received by the Frenchman, and that several articles of the Lady's father's property was found in his box, (which however, appeared to have been conveyed to him under the directions of the Lady), Mr. Bond committed him to Clerkenwell prison; and consigned the lady to the care of her father. *The Times, 21 August 1793*

Tuesday the Frenchman, with whom a Physician's daughter eloped on Friday last, was brought up for re-examination at the Public Office, Bow-street; the charge preferred against him was, that having receiv'd certain articles of plate, and some few trinkets, the property of the fair fugitive's father, knowing them to have been stolen; however, upon the examination it appeared, that the whole of the articles found in the prisoner's possession, were the distinct property of the young lady; the prisoner was in consequence discharged. *Norfolk Chronicle, 24 August 1793*

On the 25th ult. was married at Graitna-Green [sic], Mr. E. Ward, of Castle-Sowerby [Cumberland], dry salter, to Miss Bell, of Kingmoor, near Carlisle; the envied hope of many wooers. On the night appointed by the lovers for the elopement, the bridegroom went from Carlisle to Kingmoor in a chaise. On arrival, he was greatly mortified to find that the father had obtained intelligence of Miss's intention, and had locked every door to prevent her escape. What cannot love devise? they found means to converse through a key-hole, and she informed her lover, that if he could get a rope, and ascend the top of the house, his attempt would be crowned with success; for he might easily *draw her up the chimney*. A rope was accordingly procured, and the lover, assisted by the wings of love, ascended, and enlarged the lady; who, though *besmeared with soot*, retained her charms and vows; and the knot was tied without further interruption.

Northampton Mercury, 2 November 1793

Edward Ward, aged thirty-three, married Margaret Bell, twenty-five, at Stanwix, Cumberland on 26 September 1793. The chimney escapade sounds unlikely.

1794

The late Major Halliday has left one daughter. This young lady eloped some time since with an officer, to Gretna Green, where the young couple contrived to effect their purpose, though closely pursued... but the Major would never be prevailed upon to see them after their return, though they resided but a short distance from the Leasowes [pastures]: it is probable, however, they will enjoy the late Major's large fortune, after the decease of Lady Jane. *Hereford Journal, 9 July 1794*

1795

The following is given as a caution to young women against the too frequent custom of their following private soldiers: the daughter of a respectable publican in Leicester, was seduced by an Irish recruit quartered at her father's house, and eloped with him to Scotland, from thence to Dublin, where he robbed her of her cloaths, and left her almost naked and penniless. She subsisted in Ireland by begging from whence she returned to England, and continued the same means for subsistence. A few days since she reached Stafford, and was discovered in a most deplorable situation in a hole near the soldier's guard room, after having been four days almost without subsistence, and was nearly frozen to death. Her feet began to mortify, and she must have perished but for the humanity of the Chief Magistrate of the place, who sent her to the infirmary.

Ipswich Journal, 28 February 1795

This story is probably apocryphal. See also page 192.

1796

EXETER ASSIZES. TYLER versus DEYHURST. Breach of Promise of Marriage. This was a cause that exhibited a remarkable instance of female inconstancy: The action was brought by the plaintiff against Miss E. M. Deyhurst, to recover a compensation in damages for a breach of promise of marriage.

The circumstances of the case, as they were disclosed in evidence, were these: The plaintiff, a young man of a respectable family and connections, had for some time been in the habits of intimacy with the defendant's family, whose relations and connections were equally respectable. In consequence of this friendly intercourse, the plaintiff had constant access to the defendant, and used frequently to accompany her to balls, and other places of innocent amusement. The politeness and attention of the plaintiff on these occasions were merely in conformity to the habits of a polished life, having at that time felt no other regard for her, than what he entertained for the sex in general. The lady, however, was not quite so indifferent with respect to the plaintiff, for she had conceived a violent affection for him, which it was impossible for her to conceal from her relations, although it was, as yet, unknown to the plaintiff. The plaintiff having occasion to go into Yorkshire on very particular business, became acquainted with a rich farmer's daughter, to whom he paid his addresses. At this time, the affection of the defendant had rather increased than diminished by the absence of the plaintiff, and fearing she should never be united to him in wedlock, yielded to despair, became delirious, and her life was pronounced in danger. Of her unhappy condition, and the cause of it, information was given to the plaintiff who, touched with compassion, agreed to marry her. The defendant soon recovered, and appeared perfectly happy in the contemplation of her intended marriage; but about four days prior to the time fixed for its solemnization, to the unspeakable surprise of the plaintiff and others, she eloped from her father's house with another man, to whom she was married in London about a month afterwards. Two witnesses were called but as neither of them could prove the promise of marriage, the plaintiff was nonsuited [the case was stopped for lack of evidence]. *Hampshire Chronicle, 17 September 1796*

On Monday se'ennight Miss S., second daughter of Mr. S., a member of the House of Commons, eloped from her father's house in Mary[le]bone, with Lieut. R. of the royal navy. As the lady under the will of her grandmother is entitled to an immense fortune, a pursuit was next morning begun, not by land to Gretna Green, for the son of Neptune, on this occasion, preferred his own element to all others, and hoisting the main-sail of a large pleasure-boat, which he hired for the purpose, was wafted down the Thames the first stage as far as Gravesend. There he was obliged to wait for the tide, and here just as the tide had half flooded, he was overtaken by the lady's brother and some more friends, who had, by the treachery of her maid (who refused to trust her sweet person to the water) discovered the nautical track the Lieutenant took. Our hero received them, four in number, politely on board, and having his bark well manned, he weighed anchor standing for a little island called Old Haven, between Gravesend and the Nore, where he put the four gentlemen on shore, and wishing them a good day, pursued his voyage with a favourable wind. From Old Haven, the gentlemen did not get away until the Wednesday following, when they were put on board a collier, and arrived in London on Friday at about 12 o'clock. *Hampshire Chronicle, 19 November 1796*

Thursday last a party set out from Worcester on a matrimonial trip for Gretna Green; forgetting that Love should have wings, the gentleman very deliberately travelled with a chaise and pair only accompanied by his intended lady and his own sister, well loaded with trunks, containing dresses &c. As soon as the elopement was discovered a brisk pursuit was made in a chaise and four which overtook the tardy lovers at Newcastle, and brought back the lady – her name is said to be Hall, and that of the Gentleman Bailey. *Bath Chronicle and Weekly Gazette, 24 November 1796*

1797

An elopement of a curious nature lately took place in the fashionable world. The son of a well known and popular Alderman lately eloped with a young Lady, aged about fifteen, the daughter of an Officer of rank and fortune in India. The young Gentleman's age is seventeen. They were pursued by the brother of the Lady, who is a year older than his sister, attended by his footboy. They were overtaken at an inn on the road to Gretna, and the intended bride brought back. We understand, that a marriage is immediately to take place, with the consent of the friends of both parties. *Derby Mercury, 2 February 1797*

On Monday se'ennight, Lieutenant [Willoughby Bryant] Stawell, of the Chatham Division of Marines, recruiting at Trowbridge, Wilts[hire], eloped with Miss Steel [Frances Maria Still], daughter of the late Mr. Steel, Clothier, of Hilperton; a young lady possessed of every mental and personal accomplishment which can possibly decorate the human mind. Mr. Stawell took her from the back window of an apartment in her mother's dwelling-house, and immediately went for Gretna Green, in a chaise and four. *Hereford Journal, 24 May 1797*

On Wednesday the 6th instant, Miss D—, daughter of a respectable Magistrate for the County of Essex, eloped from her father's house with Mr. C— H—, son of a Gentleman in one of the Public Offices. At twelve o'clock at noon, the lady went out of the parlour, telling her mother she was going to dress, but instead of doing so, went into the garden, got out the back way, crossed a field, and was helped over the pales by two gentlemen, who handed her into a post-chaise, and drove to Epping, where Mr H— was waiting in a post-chaise and four... they took the road to Gretna Green and have not since been heard of. Miss D— is a very elegant and accomplished young lady, about twenty years of age, and when twenty-one, will have an annuity of £900 per annum. *Derby Mercury, 21 September 1797*

1798

Wednesday morning, in consequence of a late elopement, a meeting took place in Hyde Park, between the Hon. Capt. Butler of the 12 dragoons, and —Bryer, Esq. Capt. Butler received his antagonist's fire, and discharged his pistol in the air, after which the business was amicably settled. *Ipswich Journal, 5 May 1798*

A Miss L—, a young lady of sixteen, and of immense fortune, eloped a few days since from a boarding-school, near one of the most fashionable squares, with a footman. It is supposed they are gone for Gretna Green.

Bath Chronicle and Weekly Gazette, 8 November 1798

A young Lady of respectable connections in Leicester-square, eloped yesterday with a Knight of the Shoulder-Knot, whom she contrived to meet at a most infamous house, in Old Round-Court, Strand, where she solicited her parents to let her go, under the pretext of its being a dancing school for young ladies.

Northampton Mercury, 17 November 1798

1799

A young Lady whose heart seems to be of the *muslin* kind, at once tender and inflammable, eloped on Thursday night, from the fashionable end of town with her *Guardian*. The great disparity between *seventeen* and *fifty* induced her mother, with a view to obstruct the matrimonial propensities of the love-sick fair, to doom her to solitary confinement in a penitentiary bed-chamber, on the third floor. Thither the eyes of her loving Argus followed her. A faithful servant was the confidant of his amour, and to his sagacity was consigned the arduous task of liberating the fair captive. A tree, planted by love, raised its lusty branches almost close to the chamber window; to which with their friendly aid, *John* mounted at midnight, and the adventurous damsel consigning herself to his care descended in safety. *January*, no doubt was at the foot of the tree, with the lovely *May* in its boughs. Alas! no such thing, he was snoring in bed. The faithful 'Squire, however, soon awoke him to his good fortune; and a Chaise being in readiness, they immediately set out for Gretna Green. The Gentleman is a naval officer; the young Lady, when of age, will be entitled to a fortune of £15,000.

Derby Mercury, 30 May 1799

On Thursday last, a young lady eloped from Kensington, with an Hibernian youth, who brought her to his apartments in Brook Street, where not having money enough to discharge the post-boy, some words ensued; in consequence of which, the boy went back to inform the lady's friends of the circumstance, who arrived about five o'clock on Friday morning, when a regular siege commenced. About ten her brother found means to enter the house, and finding the Irishman had made his escape the back way, he conducted her (to her no small mortification) through the crowd to a hackney coach, which was in waiting.

Oxford Journal, 31 August 1799

A second elopement has taken place at Southampton; the parties are a Medical Gentleman and a young Ward of good fortune. Impatient of the consent of her Guardians and Law delays, the lovers set sail last week for the Island of Jersey; and there is much reason to fear Mr C. and his bride elect have been taken by the French. *Hereford Journal, 25 September 1799*

1800

A daughter of Mr. Macnamara, who became known to the Public many years ago by the address with which he carried off and married the heiress of Mr. Jones, a rich Lawyer, recently eloped with a young Clergyman, who was the domestic tutor of her brothers. The married couple, it seems had contrived to get the Banns published in due course, and escaped from the Family Mansion before any body had risen. At present it seems the family are much incensed against the wedded Pair, but as the bridegroom belongs to so respectable a class of the community, is a man of learning and talents, and as the *Conjugal Fugitives* can plead a *Parental Precedent* in their behalf, it is supposed that a reconciliation will soon take place, particularly as Mr. Macnamara is distinguished by an open, generous, and manly character. *Derby Mercury, 9 January 1800*

In an advertisement, addressed to a Young Lady who eloped, she is *most earnestly* requested to return to her most disconsolate Parents; but it is added, that, if she does not choose to come herself, she is most particularly desired to send the Key of the *Tea chest!* *Staffordshire Advertiser, 31 May 1800*

1801

The present season augurs favourably for the wedlock-smiths at Gretna Green; no less than four couples have been riveted together at the Hymeneal temple at that place within these few days. One couple were from Martinique, and were accompanied by four gentlemen of the same place. They spoke English so indifferently, that it was with difficulty they could make themselves understood on the road; but when they reached the place of destination, they produced before Mr. Long (by whom the ceremony was performed) an infallible interpreter (thirty guineas) and the connubial chain was forged without the least loss of time. *31 October 1801, Lancaster Gazetteer*

On Tuesday a motion was made in the Court of Chancery, for an order for the appearance of William Woodman, to answer for having eloped with Elizabeth Bathurst, a ward of the Court, only 16 years old. It was stated, that Woodman was a person of low condition, and usually employed as a journeyman silversmith – it was supposed he either had or would marry the young lady. The elopement had taken place on the 3d of December, and the parties contrived to get on board a smuggling vessel, in which they proceeded to Guernsey. They were traced, and an application was made to Sir Hugh Dalrymple, the Governor of that Island, to adopt the necessary measures for securing the lady, and the person with whom she had absconded. They however, effected their escape, and returned to London, and it was only on Monday night that the place of their retreat had been discovered. The Lord Chancellor made an order for the appearance of the parties, and in obedience thereto, they yesterday attended the Court. Mr. Woodman preferred an affidavit in his behalf, in which he stated, that he had been apprenticed to a respectable tradesman of the name of Walsh, at Plymouth; that he had duly served the period of his apprenticeship, and was now of the age of 23 years; that his father was a man of property, and had retired from business, possessed of lands and tenements to a considerable amount; that in the mouth of February last he became acquainted with Miss Bathurst, whose father in his life-time was an eminent bookseller, at Temple-bar; that a mutual attachment was the consequence of their acquaintance; that they determined to marry, and to accomplish their design went to the Island of Guernsey, where they were married by a Clergyman of that place. He added that he had some reason to believe Miss Bathurst was a young lady of property; but did not know she was a Ward of Chancery, or possessed of the sum of £30,000.

The Chancellor said, he understood Mr. Woodman's father and brother had assisted his elopement with Miss Bathurst, and accompanied them to Guernsey... [illegible]. His Lordship ordered Mr. [Woodman]... [illegible] Master should report on... [illegible] the circumstances of his marriage; and he assured him, if he suffered his wife to visit him it would considerably protract the period of his imprisonment. He also said, if his father and brother should appear to have been implicated with him, he should likewise commit them to the Fleet.

The appearance and manners of the bridegroom furnish some apology for the young lady's disregard of the restrains imposed by the circumstances of her fortune. With respect to herself, though only sixteen years of age, her figure indicates her arrival at a period of more maturity. Mr. Woodman was conveyed to the Fleet. *Exeter Flying Post, 31 December 1801*

On 8 January 1803 the Mirror of the Times announced that William Woodman and Elizabeth Bathurst had married at Walsingham in Norfolk: 'The repetition of the ceremony is occasioned by the apprehension of some legal informality when it was first performed.'

1802

At the York Assizes, on Saturday, a trial came on which has, for the last eighteen months, interested the whole county of York, and formed the subject of conversation at every tea table in every female circle. It was a bill of indictment preferred by Bacon Frank, Esq., a very active and valuable magistrate, residing near Doncaster, against Mr. Hewitt, a Gentleman who has made a large fortune in the West Indies, but now residing near Doncaster; and Colonel Sowerby, of the Artillery, an elderly gentleman residing in Doncaster, for a conspiracy to make Mr. Frank's son elope and marry the daughter of the said Colonel Sowerby.

It was stated by Mr. Serjeant Cokell for the plaintiff that Frank, jun. was a young man of weak intellects, and that he had been ensnared into the marriage with the young lady by the defendants, and that the object was the great fortune to which he was heir. A number of witnesses, chiefly post-boys and persons on the road to Gretna Green, were called to prove the case; but nothing was made out to establish a conspiracy.

Mr. PARKE, for the defendants, reprobated the prosecution in the strongest terms, and represented the conduct of the defendants as perfectly proper. He denied that young Frank was of weak intellects, and said that the marriage was sufficiently equal, and turned out very happy.

Before the defendants' witnesses were called the prosecution was withdrawn, and the defendants acquitted.

Morning Chronicle, 18 March 1802

Mary Frances Sowerby, twenty-six, and Edward Richard Frank, twenty-one, married at Doncaster on 8 March 1801. Edward later became a Church of England minister. The marriage produced at least three children. Edward died in 1834 and Mary Frances four years later.

A worthy family, in the West end of the town, are plunged into the greatest distress, by the elopement of a young lady of sixteen; placed under their care by her parents in India, who contrived to go off with *an Irishman,* on the wrong side of *fifty,* a short time since. Every search has been made for her hitherto without effect. The seducer has written to the lady's guardians, telling them, that if they would settle a handsome annuity on her, as he has no fortune of his own, he will *marry* her.

Morning Chronicle, 22 May 1802

The daughter of a Lady of Fashion, on Tuesday last, eloped from her mother's house at Isleworth [Middlesex], with an Officer of the Dragoons, on a matrimonial expedition to Scotland. The *fair fugitive* can hardly be excused on the score of juvenile indiscretion, as she is on the *wrong side of thirty.* Her military escort is only *nineteen.* *Hampshire Telegraph, 27 December 1802*

1803

Mary and Thomas Pearce were illegitimate children of Mr. Pearce, a London brewer who died in 1803. His widow Isabel or Elizabeth, almost immediately remarried after his death, becoming Mrs. Locker Wainwright. On 22 August 1803 at St. Luke's in Finsbury, north London, Mary, who was then nineteen, said to be of 'weak understanding' and entitled to £15,000 when of age, married her stepmother's husband's uncle, 64-year-old John Locker or Lockyer, an Irish farmer. Mrs. Wainwright, Locker Wainwright and John Locker found themselves in the Court of Chancery and thereafter in the Court of King's Bench, charged with conspiracy.

COURT OF CHANCERY. The several parties who on a former day were ordered to attend his Lordship on Thursday, in the matter of the elopement of Miss Pearce, a Ward of the Court, with a person of the name of John Locker, appeared.

From the various affidavits read, it was shewn that... shortly after her [Mary Pearce's] father's death... his widow became acquainted with a very young man in one of the Theatres, and in a few days afterwards married him, whose name is John Locker Wainwright; that he is the nephew of the person who eloped with

Miss Pearce, and that her elopement was favoured and planned by Mrs. Wainwright, who assisted Locker in having a post-chaise in waiting for the purpose, near the house of her guardian, Mr. Crutchfield, a very respectable Gentleman, living in the neighbourhood of Teddington. A variety of collateral matters appeared in aggravation of this case; the Clergyman who published the banns, and married them, the Parish Clerk and Sexton, who were the only attesting witnesses, and Mrs. Wainwright, together with the Ward were all present. Wainwright, (who is confined for debt in the custody of the Sheriff of the county of Surry [sic]) not appearing, and his Lordship having maturely considered the whole of the circumstances of the case, the disparagement of ages in the parties, and the difference of property, and denominating it altogether a base and mercenary transaction, said, that he trusted he should be able to render at least some part of the scheme abortive, and he was resolved to prevent the commission of the like offence in future: for the present, his order to keep Locker in close custody should continue: and as he did not believe that the matter of imprisonment merely would operate as a sufficient and adequate punishment to the persons especially concerned in the foul transaction, he should order that all the papers and the case be laid forthwith before the Attorney General, for the purpose of instituting a criminal, and he trusted, effectual prosecution for a conspiracy. In the mean time, he directed that the matter should remain over till the next Seal Day, whereon the same persons were ordered to attend.

Derby Mercury, 8 September 1803

...WILLIAM COLLET, a post-boy, living with Mr. HODSON at Richmond, said, that on the 6th of August, LOCKER and WAINWRIGHT came to his Master's Yard, and ordered a post-chaise. They also asked for a short ladder which was in the yard, which was tied under the perch. They first went to Mr. WAINWRIGHT's house at Richmond, and took up Mrs. L. WAINWRIGHT, and MARY COX, a servant. They then drove to Bushy Park, when the men left them a short time; afterwards, Miss PEARCE made her appearance, and she was then put into the chaise, and she, MARY COX, and Mr. LOCKER, was driven by the witness to London.

MARY COX, the servant, stated the same as the last witness, and added further, that from London she accompanied them to Leicestershire, and from thence to Gretna Green, where they were married. On their return, they went to the house of Mr. LOCKER WAINWRIGHT, at Richmond...

The proceedings in Chancery, appointing Mr. CRUTCHFIELD guardian, were next read — as were also the two letters found in Miss PEARCE's desk. They contained copies for her to write to an Attorney, in order to instruct him to get Mr. LOCKER appointed her guardian.

Mr. BURROWES, for the defendant LOCKER, addressed the Jury, and contended that his client was a fit match for the lady in every respect, except in point of age, which was a consideration for herself alone — that he was a gentleman, and a man of fortune in Ireland. To prove this, he called Mr. FOSTER, the Speaker of the late Irish House of Commons. He stated, that he had known LOCKER for 25 years, but did not speak with much certainty as to his fortune or character. Mr. ASTLEY, a gentleman from Leicestershire, said he had known LOCKER in Ireland, where he went to buy a farm, which he considered worth £5000; but he only knew the defendant's title from himself. The Honourable Mr. POLE [William Wellesley-Pole], brother of [Richard] the Marquis of WELLESLEY, said, the defendant LOCKER held a farm of the Marquis, under a perpetual lease. He was in arrears when the Marquis went to India, but he had since paid it off. On further examination it appeared that he had paid it off when he sold the farm. Mr. ERSKINE then addressed the Jury for the other defendants, and defended them on the ground that the whole was the work of Mr. LOCKER alone, and that the plan of the marriage was entirely arranged between Mr. LOCKER and Miss PEARCE, without the knowledge or privity of the other defendants.

Morning Post, 23 February 1804

Court of King's Bench, Thu. June 14... Mr. BURROWS addressed the court on behalf of LOCKYER, the husband, and urged that he used no undue influence to gain the young lady's affection; that she was a sensible girl, within two months of twenty, and consequently, capable of forming a judgment of what would make her happy in life... *Morning Post, 15 June 1804*

The defendants were sentenced to eighteen months' imprisonment. Mary Pearce left her husband within a few months of marriage, and there followed years of legal wranglings about how provision was to be made for her. Her brother Thomas's relationship was also the subject of legal action. He and Mary Farmer, a widow, were prevented from marrying by an order in 1804 of the Lord Chancellor, Lord Eldon, but were eventually united in 1809. Thomas died in 1820. John Locker died in 1825 and Mary Pearce in 1840.

The case of Mr. [Barkham] Cony, a ward in chancery, came on to be heard in that court on Saturday last. This was an application on the part of the relatives of a gentleman, named Cony, to set aside his marriage with Miss Elizabeth Franklin, he being a minor and a ward in Chancery at the time of such marriage. It appeared that this gentleman was only 17 years of age, that he possessed a large property in the county of Norfolk, had become enamoured of the above lady, the daughter of an innkeeper at Downham, the neighbourhood of his residence, and finally had expressed his determination of marrying her. It was in vain his relatives endeavoured to dissuade him from his purpose; he was suddenly missed, an elopement took place, the parties came to London, a licence was obtained, and a clandestine marriage was the consequence. His Lordship... ordered the attendance of the girl's father, her sister, and a gentleman named Palmer, the friend of Mr. Cony. The father persisted in his having forbid the marriage, the sister, that she knew nothing of the matter, and the friend, that he had used his best influence in dissuading Mr. Cony from the match. *Norfolk Chronicle, 27 August 1803*

After the Lord Chancellor annulled their first marriage, which took place at St. Botolph Without Bishopsgate in London, Barkham Cony (or Coney) and Elizabeth Franklin were remarried in October 1804.

1804

Early on Thursday morning Mr. Garnham Steadman, son of Mr. J. Steadman, of Ixworth [Norfolk], eloped with the beautiful daughter of Mr. Boldero, an opulent farmer of the same place; Mr. B. being informed of the circumstance immediately pursued the flying couple; when, by the carelessness of the driver, the chaise unfortunately upset, and Mr. Boldero was so dreadfully bruised that he lingered but two hours when he expired. The memory of this unfortunate gentleman will be held dear by all those who knew him, from his unbounded liberality, his goodness as a Christian, a husband, a neighbour and a friend.

Ipswich Journal, 14 January 1804

Four days later, the Bury and Norwich Post published a correction. 'We have the pleasure to inform our readers, that the report of the death of Mr. Boldero, of Ixworth, by the overturning of a chaise, together with all the circumstances leading thereto (inserted in a neighbouring print) are totally void of foundation.'

Last Friday morning, about three o'clock, a Lieutenant in the Navy eloped with the daughter of an eminent Jew at Portsmouth. They had left Portsmouth several hours before their flight was discovered, when the father of the young lady, accompanied by a friend, pursued them in a chaise and four, taking the London road. On his arrival at Kingston he met with the post-boy who drove the lovers to town, who told him he drove the happy pair to the Golden Cross, Charing Cross; but the father thinking it most advisable to procure the assistance of the Police, drove to the Public Office, Bow Street, and procured two officers to assist him in his pursuit. They went to the Golden Cross, but all the information that could be gained was, that the lovers remained there but a short time and went away in a hackney coach, and no trace could be had of the coach. It being suspected that application would be made at Doctor's Commons [a civil law court], for a license, in the course of Saturday, several persons were set to watch, with the Bow Street Officers; and, about two o'clock, the gallant Officer applied for a license, when the Officers took him into custody, and conveyed him to the father, who proposed, if he would pay all expences [sic], not to prosecute him — to which the lover was reluctantly obliged to agree, and to tell, that the object of his affections was at lodgings in Fludyer Street, Westminster; where the fair damsel was found, and returned, very unwillingly, with her father to Portsmouth.

Oxford Journal, 22 December 1804

1805

In early 1805 Julia Maria Petre, the daughter of Lord Petre, eloped with her brothers' music tutor, Stephen Phillips, a Roman Catholic.

...every precaution, such as searching the mail-coaches, and stationing proper people to watch on the great Northern Road, have been resorted to. The lady will shortly become possessed of a very great fortune. *Morning Post, 27 February 1805*

...the attachment has been a growing one for some time, and is said to have been discovered by Lady P. who acquainted her husband with it, and his Lordship in consequence, gave the gentleman intimation that it was his intention to procure him a more eligible situation. The tutor apprehensive that the scent had been discovered, hastened to secure her flight without delay...

Morning Post, 28 February 1805

Julia's flight attracted the attention of Marianne Stanhope, the daughter of Walter Stanhope-Spencer of Cannon Hall, who wrote to her brother John Stanhope on 1 March: 'The Elopement and distress in the House of Petre has been the chief subject of conversation for the last few days... It is said they are at Worcester and married only by a Catholic Priest. However, Lord and Lady P. are gone there and it is expected she will be brought back to-night. They can do nothing but get her married to the man at Church. She is 18, he 30, and no Gentleman. She was advertised and 20 guineas [£21] reward offered to anyone who could give an account of the stray sheep. It is a sad History. What misery this idle girl has caused her parents, and probably ensured her own for life.' Two days later, Marianne added: 'He is a very low man, quite another class, always dined with the children.' Quoted from A.M.W. Stirling, 'The Letter-bag of Lady Elizabeth Spencer-Stanhope', Vol. 1 (1913, London: John Lane).

Mr. Lessie, the RC priest, who married the Hon. Miss Petre to Mr. Philips, is arrived in town to explain to Lord Petre the deception which was practised upon him by the lovers, who assured him that they had previously been married agreeably to the rites of the Church of England, which does not appear to have been the case. Lady Petre continues inconsolable and her worthy Lord is not less unhappy on the occasion.

Caledonian Mercury, 9 March 1805

...the man's name is Phillips; he is the son of a village barber, who lives rent-free in a cottage built on the estate of W. Sheldon Esq. at Braine, in Warwickshire. The son, who is a Catholic, but not a priest, was educated through the benevolence of Mr. S. at Douay [Douai], in Flanders, and from his exemplary conduct was afterwards recommended to his patron Lord Petre, as a preceptor to his son. The fugitives, after quitting Bucknam, never stopped til they reached Oxford, where they were married by a priest according to the Catholic ceremony; and they were previously married conformably in the rites of the Est[ablished] church; and in the case the marriage is illegal will subject the Catholic priest to the pains and penalties attached to daring a violation of a criminal statute. *Leeds Intelligencer, 11 March 1805*

Lord Petre, with infinite goodness of heart and parental affection, has pardoned his daughter's disobedience. Though his Lordship has not yet condescended to see her in person, yet he kindly corresponds with her, and countenances visits to his friends and noble relatives; he has also made the young couple a very handsome allowance for their present subsistence, and encouraged them, as they are deserving, to hope for much from his future generosity and condescension.

Oxford Journal, 13 July 1805

A perfect reconciliation has at length taken place between Lord Petre and the successful fugitives. The happy interview took place at the House of Sir J. Throgmorton, on Thursday se'ennight, through the good offices of that gentleman and the Hon. Mrs. Creevy. *Derby Mercury, 15 August 1805*

Miss F[ranks], a Jewess of great expectation, eloped from her relations near Barnes Green [south-west of London], on Thursday last, with Capt. W. of the Navy.

Bury and Norwich Post, 17 April 1805

The young Jewess that lately eloped from Barnes Green has no fortune independent of her father, who is inflexible. This young lady is related to the Miss F. [Isabella Bell Franks] who married the eldest son [William Henry Cooper] of the late Sir GREY COOPER [in 1787]; and it is said her father had destined her to marry a relation she disliked, a young Jew, possessing a considerable property and large expectancies.

Morning Post, 20 April 1805

The young and beautiful Jewess, who eloped with Captain W. of the navy was made a happy bride, as soon as she and her gallant enamorato had crossed the Tweed: her opulent father promises to forgive her, provided that she will return, and receive the absolution of the Synagogue.

Aberdeen Journal, 1 May 1805

Margaret Franks, the daughter of Jacob Henry Franks and Margaret Roper, married Henry Waring at the church of St. George, Hanover Square on 4 April 1805. They went on to have at least ten children.

FIG.31 Grandmamma's Elopement, detail from *The Graphic* (Christmas, 1878). After the taste for clandestine marriage declined in the late 19th century, it was viewed primarily as a romantic escapade.

"None but the brave deserves the fair" —A curious adventure occurred in the Barton Hoy [a hoy is a small coastal sailing vessel] last Tuesday morning. A gentleman, 18 years of age, resident not 100 miles from Eckington, near Sleaford, in Lincolnshire, eloped with a young lady of the same place, aged 16 years, (*Oh! tempora; Oh! mores!*) The fugitives arrived safe on board the hoy, and were congratulating themselves exceedingly and rather loudly on having eluded the vigilance of Argus and Duenna, —when lo! at the moment the hoy was putting off, a chaise drove up to the door of the inn; one of the passengers, a young man, rushed out of the vehicle, and in a small boat made after the hoy; on coming up with which, he exclaimed with great exultation and clapping of hands, (to the no small diversion of the passengers,): "They are here, they are here!" This was addressed to his fellow-traveller, who proved to be the father of the young lady, and who joining the other, instantly boarded the hoy and separated the lovers. The lady shewed much spirit and attachment to her swain, and remonstrated very warmly, but the latter suffered the prize to be borne off by (it is conjectured) his rival, without uttering a word. The whole party came over in the hoy to Hull, and at the recommendation of one of the passengers, participated in a conciliatory dinner at the inn; after which they returned by way of York, Jerry Sneak driving their rear guard.

Leeds Intelligencer, 22 July 1805

An elopement took place on Friday se'ennight from a villa near Croydon [Surrey]. The seducer was a visitant in the family, of 30 years of age. The deluded female is a child in frocks, 14 years of age, and of remarkably childish appearance. All the trace that has yet been made of the transit is, that on Sunday morning last persons answering the description took a hackney-coach from the Stones End in the Borough [south of London Bridge], and putting in their baggage a few light boxes and bundles, drove to Gracechurch-street, where they alighted and put the baggage in the bar, as if waiting to go by a stage-coach. They soon shifted from thence in another hackney-coach, and drove off; where to has baffled all endeavours to trace them, although the parents, who are inconsolable for her loss, have offered a very handsome reward for intelligence of them. *Morning Post, 11 October 1805*

On Friday a young lady about fifteen years of age, and a gentleman about thirty, went to the Roebuck Inn, at Turnham Green [west of London], where they ordered supper. From the description of a runaway pair, whom the landlord had seen advertised, he had a suspicion his customers were the persons. On Saturday morning he communicated to them his suspicions and insisted upon their going with him to Bow Street, where they underwent a private examination, when the lady proved to be the one who had lately eloped from her friends at Croydon. The magistrate in consequence ordered her to be detained till he had communicated the information to her friends. The gentleman not being the party who eloped with her was discharged. *Oxford Journal, 19 October 1805*

On Sunday morning the son of a wholesale linen draper, near Watling Street, eloped with the daughter of a wealthy merchant, near East Square, in the Kent Road [south London]; on their way to Guildford [Surrey] they were overtaken by the lady's father, and some of his friends, who had set off in pursuit of the fugitives. The rencounter had likely to have proved a very serious one, as the enraged parent attacked the young gentleman with such determined violence, as not only to drag him from the post chaise, but to inflict upon him a severe drubbing with a cudgel. [The young man was preparing to die] when the young lady called her father aside, reminding him that she had left home for more than twelve hours; that a night had passed in the interval since she had determined to become a wife; and that it would neither contribute to her happiness nor her honour to prevent the match, since things had gone so far. The parent took the hint, and was, after a moment's recollection, as desirous to see the nuptial ceremony performed as he was before resolute to prevent it. The parties all returned to town, and yesterday the happy pair was joined in holy wedlock, when the Lady confessed that the hint she had thrown out was nothing more than an innocent stratagem to gain her parent's consent, and that her own honour and his reputation were unsullied. *Oxford Journal, 12 October 1805*

An elopement attended with circumstances of a distressing nature, took place in the neighbourhood of Hull about a fortnight ago. A young lady who was placed at a boarding-school, not many miles from Hull, and had just entered her fifteenth year, in the middle of the night rose from the bed where she slept along with her sister, and notwithstanding some other ladies slept in the same room, escaped out of a one pair of stairs [first floor] window, without being discovered, taking along with her a great part of her cloathes. An officer, late in the third Lincoln militia, is supposed to have been waiting for her in a single horse chaise, which he had previously hired at Hull, whither he brought her very early in the morning. A vessel having just sailed for London, they procured an open boat and followed her into the roads, intending to take their passage in her, but the Captain suspecting it to be for some improper purpose, by their being so urgent at so early an hour, refused to take them on board. In consequence they were obliged to cross to Barton, in the open boat, where they arrived about one o'clock in the afternoon, having been upon the water between eight and nine hours, without refreshment. The girl went in the mail coach from Barton to London, the officer going an outside passenger. They reached London on Saturday morning, and were pursued by the lady's friends, who did not arrive however till the evening of that day, and were unable to discover the retreat of the fugitives. A correspondence it appears had been carried on by them for some time, through the medium of a confidential person, unknown to any of the young lady's friends. The infamous villain who has thus deeply injured a respectable family is between 30 and 40 years of age. This is not the first transaction of this kind of which he has been guilty, while in that neighbourhood, and we are sorry to say, that he has succeeded too well in similar attempts upon the unsuspecting and unguarded victims. Indeed against such his aim has particularly been directed. Such conduct ought to draw down the indignation of every person, and consign the author of it to that infamy and contempt which he so justly merits.

Leeds Intelligencer, 21 October 1805

1806

The daughter of a wealthy Jew merchant in the City, some evenings since, eloped from the house of a gentleman in the neighbourhood of Bloomsbury Square, where she had been invited to a large party. A young gentleman, who was likewise there, is also missing. *Morning Post, 6 January 1806*

Two young ladies of fortune eloped from the neighbourhood of Walworth [Southwark], last week, with two old gentlemen at least treble their age. Such appears to be the rage of the present day! *Morning Post, 13 January 1806*

Saturday last, a young lady of Leicester, of much respectability and fortune, eloped with an attorney of considerable eminence in the same town. During the absence of the family to a dinner party, she contrived to remove all her cloaths [that is, she packed her clothes], but being observed, information was given to her parents the same evening.

Her father sat up all night in his boots, determined to disappoint any bold intruder; but in the morning, about nine o'clock, being rather overcome with sleep, the lady took advantage of the moment and leaped the garden wall and ran through the beast market, to the great astonishment of all the two and four-legged animals, without either cap or hat, to the house of her gallant, from whence they proceeded to church, got married, and immediately set off for the metropolis.

Morning Post, 7 February 1806

The Gentleman in Harley-street [in the West End of London], who has recovered his runaway daughter from his Coachman, with whom she recently eloped, asked her what she had to say for her conduct? She answered, that she had long thought from his affection to his horses, and the manner of managing his reins, that JOHN would make a loving husband, and therefore she was determined to accompany him through every stage of his life: to which her father replied, "Well, girl! then so it must be, but I fear you'll soon find, that you have got on the wrong box!" *Bury and Norwich Post, 23 July 1806*

1807

On Wednesday morning, Mr. Gill, druggist, of Sherborne [Dorset], set off from town, in a post chaise and four, for Weymouth, accompanied by Miss Wadham, an heiress, aged seventeen years. They were followed by the young lady's guardian, in another chaise and four; but, from the precautions taken by the lovers, much time had elapsed before the pursuit commenced, and the guardian in consequence arrived at Weymouth just an hour after the Guernsey packet, with the fugitives on board, had sailed with a fair wind, which has doubtless ere this wafted them to the haven of Matrimony. *Hereford Journal, 28 January 1807*

HORSHAM [Sussex Assizes], Tuesday, March 17. CROWN SIDE. James Vaughan Everell [Everall], a genteel young man, aged 24 was indicted for maliciously pointing a pistol, loaded with ball, at Victor Amadée Raymond, and pulling the trigger, with intent to murder him...

The Prosecutor, Mr. Raymond, [for] many years kept a school of great respectability, at Lewes, in this County [Sussex], and the Defendant came into his family in January, 1805, as an usher. While he was there, he paid his addresses to the Prosecutor's daughter [Maria Petronelle Raymond], but against the knowledge of the Prosecutor. They at length eloped together, and were married. The young woman, however, lived with him but a short time, being, from the ill-treatment of the prisoner, obliged again to seek the shelter of her father's house...

The Prisoner... asked his wife if she would live with him, provided he could get the means to support her? She replied that she would, if he would not misconduct himself in the manner he had hitherto done. He then requested to be left alone with his wife, which being refused, his demeanour became so outrageous, that Mr. Cripps thought it necessary to order him to be turned out of the house. He [returned] about four o'clock, and knowing the ways of the house, he gained access to the parlour door...

Victor Amadée Raymond... added, that as he was sitting at tea in the parlour he heard the door open, and supposing it was his assistant, he said, "walk in," without lifting his eyes from a letter which he was reading. But hearing a voice exclaim, "Now God d——n you," he looked up and saw the prisoner, who pulled a pistol from under his coat and snapped it at him. The pistol snapped in the pan; he attempted to wrest it from the prisoner, but the latter being the strongest prevented him, and closing the pan, he snapped it at him a second time...

The prisoner, in his defence, urged that he was driven to desperation by the prosecutor having allured the affections of his wife from him, and said that he meant to have shot himself in the presence of his wife. Verdict — GUILTY.

When he was sentenced he prayed for mercy, and desire to be sent from England for ever. *Morning Chronicle, 19 March 1807*

Maria Petronelle Raymond, twenty-two, married James Everall at All Saints, Lewes on 30 April 1805. She may not have known that a month before he joined her father's household his marriage to Sophia Hilliard in Spitalfields, London, for which banns had been read, had been cancelled. Everall's death sentence was commuted to transportation for life and he was placed aboard the prison hulk Perseus at Southampton. On 14 September he, along with others, was offered a pardon conditional on him enlisting in the Army. I have been unable to trace him after that point. The only clue is that Maria's father's will in 1820 described her as a widow. Maria died in 1869. Her baby son Robert died in December 1807.

FIG.32 Chryseis Restored To Her Father, by Francesco Bartolozzi (1786). In Greek mythology, Chryseis, a Trojan and the daughter of Chryses, was abducted and given to Agamemnon.
Yale Center for British Art, Paul Mellon Collection, B1977.14.19739.

1808

COURT OF CHANCERY. Friday, Nov. 18. Sir A. Pigott said, he held in his hand a petition from the trustees of a ward of Court, who had eloped with a Captain [John] Impey to Gretna-Green. These petitioners were a Mr. Patch, of Exeter, and Mrs. Cassel [Cazal], the mother of the ward. The petition set forth the amount of the fortune to which Miss [Fanny] Cassel was entitled on her coming of age, and which amounted to between 14 and £15,000. It also stated, that her trustees had placed her in a respectable boarding-school at Exeter, where she remained till last October, when she went to see a school-fellow of hers, a Miss Impey at Teignmouth, where she was to stay a week. While in the house of Mrs. Impey, the mother of her female friend, she was induced to set out on a matrimonial expedition to Gretna Green with Captain Impey, who was the brother to Mrs. Impey. The petition did not state that Mrs. Impey was implicated in the transaction, though it added, that Miss Impey had personally communicated the first information of the matter to Mrs. Cassel, and also that the matrimonial expedition had been talked of in the presence of Mrs. Impey. The acquaintance between the two parties was very short, not longer than the visit to Teignmouth and their relative ages were 18 and 34...

Sir S. [Samuel] Romilly appeared for Captain Impey, and observed that his client was ready to go before a Master, and make such settlement upon the young lady as the Court might think proper. He was given to understand, that his client's circumstances and rank in life were such as probably would not have been rejected, had the overtures been regularly made. Lord Chancellor —"All that I can do in this case is to order that this gentleman be committed to the Fleet Prison, and let the Master inquire what marriage has been celebrated, and report forthwith."

Kentish Gazette, 22 November 1808

Capt. Impey, R.N. son of Sir Elisha Impey, who ran away with and married Miss Cassell, a Ward of Chancery, has made his peace with the Chancellor, and is released from the Fleet prison, he having made a settlement of the lady's fortune

(£13,000) and charged his resources with £10,000 for the benefit of his wife and children. *Bury and Norwich Post, 28 December 1808*

John Impey was thirty-six when he eloped to Gretna Green with eighteen-year-old Fanny Cazal in October 1808. The couple married again at St. Bride's in London. Impey was appointed rear-admiral in 1840 and vice-admiral in 1848. He died in 1858, Fanny two years later.

1809

A most dreadful transaction has involved the family of Sir STEWKLEY SHUCKBURGH, Bart. of Upper Shuckburgh, in the county of Warwick, and the family of Lieutenant SHARPE, of the Bedford Militia, in the deepest distress. Lieut. [Philip A.] SHARPE, having paid his addressed to Miss [Caroline Anne Matilda] SHUCKBURGH, which were disapproved by the family, formed (if he should be disappointed in obtaining the object of his affections) the horrid determination of putting a period to his own, and her existence, which he carried into effect on Sunday morning last, in the plantations of Shuckburgh Park. They were overheard in earnest discourse by the butler, as if Lieutenant SHARPE was persuading her to elope with him; and, as Miss SHUCKBURGH uttered the words, No, No! he immediately heard the report of a pistol, which, in a few seconds, was succeeded by another, and they were instantly lifeless corpses!! After a most deliberate investigation of all the circumstances of this most affecting and awful event, before JOHN TOMES, Esq., and a respectable Jury, and the Rev. Mr. BROMFIELD, a Magistrate of the county, a verdict of Lunacy was given respecting Lieutenant SHARPE, and that Miss SHUCKBURGH died by his hand. Lieutenant SHARPE had been occasionally for some weeks preceding in a state of mental derangement, and in confinement.

Morning Post, 30 March 1809

Caroline Shuckburgh was buried in the churchyard at Upper Shuckburgh. Her father died four months after her murder.

1810

At Gretna Green, W. Abbott Esq., to Miss E. Kennett, both of Bath; Mr. A. was a first-rate performer on the Bath stage, and the lady possesses considerable personal, mental, and *pecuniary* attractions. *Lancaster Gazetteer, 4 July 1810*

A lady [Mary Slade Dalton] eloped on Sunday last from her father's house near Wincanton [in Hampshire], with a near relative [Robert Foster Grant]. The fair fugitive had all her life, it appears, been kept in a state of the most rigid seclusion. She had attained the age of 26 years without being permitted to have any intercourse with society. She is presumptive heiress to a property of near £200,000. The parties took the road towards London. *Morning Post, 18 August 1810*

Mary Slade Dalton, twenty-seven, and Robert Foster Grant, twenty-eight, married at the church of St. James, London. Mary died aged forty. Robert outlived her by over thirty years.

A young lady of eighteen, who resided with her parents, in King's Road, Chelsea, was missing on Sunday night last, and her absence caused the greatest anxiety and uneasiness as an elopement was never dreamt of. She, however, was discovered on Tuesday at Fulham, under the protection of a grey headed gallant of 55, a Gentleman on the Half-pay list, who resides in Grosvenor Place. The gallant was unknown to the friends of Miss T. but the Lady had been several times in the company of her paramour at Brighton which place she left about three weeks ago.

Oxford University and City Herald, 27 October 1810

1811

Last week in the parish of Leslie [in Fife, Scotland], a young girl, after the banns of marriage had been proclaimed, and the day appointed for the wedding, made an elopement with a *Chapman* [peddlar], who called at her mother's in the course of his employment. The bridegroom, as soon as the woeful tidings reached his ears, made what haste he could to recover his dear *Lucinda* [a reference to the heroine of a moral tale by Thomas Smith], and soon came up with her; but he met with a stern rebuff, neither could flowing tears, nor the softest entreaties move her to return. It is only a few weeks since another girl made an elopement from the same parish, with a *rambling* dancing master, a *bigamist*, but a fine performer in *hornpipes*. These instances, if they do not go far to refute the Turkish opinion, "that woman has no soul" at least prove that she has *spirit*. *Aberdeen Journal, 6 February 1811*

On Saturday evening, a Clerk to an Attorney in Lynn [Norfolk], went to the Bank in that town, where his master kept cash, with his Bank book, and desired to have £700. Without any other authority, they let him have it, and the business being done in a hurry, not any of the numbers of the notes were taken. On due inquiry being made, it was ascertained that a young man answering his description had arrived by the Boston coach early that morning, at the Saracen's-Head Inn, Snow-hill in company with a young lady, who was then in the Inn waiting his return, in the mean time one of the Bankers from Lynn arrived and waited with Vickery, the Bow-street officer till the described young man returned, when the Banker identified him as the person who had obtained the £700 under a pretence of being authorised by his master; upon which Vickery took him into custody, also the young Lady he had travelled with, and on searching them he found upon her, notes to the amount of near £690. Upon him he found a gold watch, chain and seals, which appeared from a bill and receipt found upon him that he had paid £50 for in London, and he had purchased several other articles. The young Lady who travelled with him is of a very respectable family and connection at Boston, and had eloped with him for the purpose of being married in London, without any knowledge of how he became possessed of the notes. *Morning Post, 11 April 1811*

1812

An unexpected elopement took place a few days since from Piccadilly, by Miss CH——D——Y withdrawing herself at night from *Ch——d——y House*, and putting herself under the protection of Mr. LAMBTON (sib of Lady ANN), setting off with him post for Gretna Green, when, 'ere this, this couple of adventrous [sic] lovers, by the matrimonial rivets of the Scottish Blacksmith, have felicitously been made one! This beautiful and accomplished young Lady is the only child of the celebrated Madame ST. ALBAN, who, dying a few years since, after her return to Paris, bequeathed her daughter £20,000. This event is not looked upon as an unpropitious one at Ch——d——y House, the Noble Lord having, as it is said, written to the amorous fugitives, kindly requesting this, on their return, they will make his seat, in Cheshire an honeymoon asylum! *Statesman, 27 January 1812*

Harriet Cholmondeley, the illegitimate daughter of George Cholmondeley, 1st Marquess of Chomondeley, by his mistress Madame Saint-Albin, was about twenty-two when she eloped with John Lambton, then twenty and therefore an 'infant'. They later married again in Cheshire. Harriet died in 1815 shortly after the birth of the youngest of her three daughters. John Lambton was raised to the peerage as Baron Durham in 1828, becoming the Earl of Durham five years later.

The only daughter of a wealthy widow landlady, near St. Neots [Cambridgeshire], eloped a few days since with a Mr. L. whose name is well known in the *chace*. A matrimonial union having met with much opposition from relations, the following ingenious stratagem was contrived:— The young lady having been given to understand it was mamma's wish she should pay a visit to some relations, who by remonstrance were to dissuade her from what was considered to be so ineligible a match, availed herself of the proposition, and set off; but it was previously agreed on by the lovers that it was more expedient for her to *oblique* for the turnpike road, and take the coach for

London, and that he should go by the Mail. They accordingly met in London, where the banns had been previously published, and were without loss of time joined in holy matrimony. The lady is only in her seventeenth year, and beautiful as young. The mother of the young lady arrived in London the following day, and as the Gordian Knot cannot be untied, we hope all parties will shortly be reconciled. *The News, 20 September 1812*

Wednesday night an interesting female, daughter of a tradesman, in Piccadilly, attempted to throw herself from the ballustrades [sic] of Blackfriars-bridge but was prevented by a Mr. Avely, of Holborn. On being interrogated as to her motive, she replied, that she had been home about a fortnight, having been seduced by a young man with whom she eloped, and who had promised her marriage, but had since left her. She was conveyed home in a coach, accompanied by Mr. A. and met with a welcome reception.

The Englishman, 1 November 1812

1813

A few days since the daughter of a respectable farmer in Norfolk eloped with one of his farming servants, but the fugitives being pursued into this neighbourhood, were discovered, and the imprudent fair one conveyed back to her distressed parents; with whom, however, she only continued till the following day, when she returned on foot to her paramour (though at the distance of more than 30 miles) and they were married next morning.

Bury and Norwich Post, 17 February 1813

The widow of a field officer, aged 58 years, eloped from her two daughters in the neighbourhood of Baker Street [London] last week, with a gallant son of Mars, a private of a light dragoon regiment, aged 22, and was led to the hymneal altar on Monday last. The lady has £800 a year, besides a handsome provision for her two daughters, provided there is no increase of family. The happy couple are spending the honeymoon at Hounslow, where they have taken a cottage. *Bury and Norwich Post, 3 February 1813*

1814

Some time since the daughter of Mr.—, Camberwell [Surrey], a young lady of great personal beauty and accomplishments, disappeared from her father's house, and no traces of her could be discovered. Her parents were overwhelmed with distress, which, however, was alleviated by their receiving a letter the day after her flight, assuring them that she was well and in safety, and that they might rest satisfied that they would hear from her again. What added to the mystery was, that the young lady had taken no cloaths with her, having left those even which she wore on the day previous to her elopement. Thus things remained for near three months, no traces of the fugitive being discovered till Friday night last, when the following curious circumstance led to the discovery of her retreat: A friend of Mr.—'s being at the Theatre on the evening in question, his attention was attracted by the appearance of two Gentlemen, who were in the adjoining box to him, one of whom he was persuaded he had before seen, but could not recollect when or where. He at length, from circumstance, was induced to suspect that the supposed Gentleman was a female, and he then recollected that the resemblance which had struck him was a resemblance to his friend's lost daughter, Miss—. After the Oratorio was over he watched them home, and saw them enter a house in Lamb's Conduit-street. He imparted his suspicions on Saturday morning to Mr.—, who anxious to satisfy his hopes and fears, immediately procured an officer to prevent opposition, and accompanied his friend to Lamb's Conduit-street, where he discovered his long lost child. A satisfactory explanation immediately took place, from which it appeared that the lady was married to the gentleman who accompanied her to the Theatre on the preceding Friday, and who was the son of a most respectable Clergyman residing in the country. Wishing to conceal his marriage from his father he prevailed on Miss— to elope with him, and to continue to wear male attire, and at the house where they lodged they passed as cousins. Immediate information of the circumstance was forwarded to the father of the gentleman, and affairs are in a fair train of amicable adjustment. *Morning Post, 16 March 1814*

This is most probably an apocryphal story used as a filler. Similar articles appeared in several newspapers over a number of years.

1815

GUILDHALL. Yesterday Mr Richard Crowther, a young gentleman of respectable connections was brought before Mr Joshua Jonathan Smith (the sitting alderman) charged with a violent outrage and assault, under the following circumstances:

It appeared that about seven o'clock on Tuesday evening, the prisoner had succeeded in enticing from her home the daughter of a most respectable merchant residing near Blackfriars bridge. The elopement was discovered, and the two sisters of the young lady sallied forth, for the purpose of rescuing her from the consequences of her imprudent flight. They had proceeded as far as Lambeth Hill [between Knightrider Street and Thames Street on the north side of the Thames], when, meeting with two boys, named Watts and Smith, they inquired if the fugitives were observed passing that way. They were replied to in the affirmative, and an offer was made to the boys that if they traced the prisoner and his companion, they should be handsomely rewarded. During this short interval, it appeared the parties had endeavoured to procure a boat to cross the river at Queenhithe, but failed.

Arriving at Earl Street, the pursuing party overtook them, when the boys and the sisters of the young lady advanced towards them, and claimed the immediate liberation of the young lady. This the prisoner resisted in such a manner as to excite the cries and screams of the two sisters, and to put the two youths already named in bodily fear; he having drawn upon them his

FIG.33 An Elopement by Moonlight by Charles B. Newhouse (1834). The standard elements of the elopement trope are included: the loyal maid, a descent by ladder, a best friend and a waiting chaise and four. See also pages 188 and 193.
Yale Center for British Art, Paul Mellon Collection. B2001.2.1026

cane sword, made several thrusts at their body, and threatened to "run the first that approached him through!" A considerable crowd had now collected and unfortunately the young lady seemed his willing companion: while he exclaimed, that none should separate him from "his lawful wife" she as violently clung to him, crying aloud, "that he was her lawful husband?"

The sisters, however, of the young lady would not stop short of her release, and the assembled spectators increasing in number as well as feeling, a general scene of confusion and outrage took place, the prisoner brandishing his sword and threatening defiance, and the sisters having their clothes torn; until at length the whole of the parties, by main fighting, reached Ludgate Hill. The assistance of the watch was now obtained, and many of the crowd having been severally threatened and attempted by the prisoner, his sword was wrested from him. He now drew forth a knife from his pocket, and threatened one of the officers of St. Bride's with destruction if he advanced towards him. This, however, was also soon after seized from his grasp, and he now called for a coach, in expectation of flight; but the crowd still increasing, the prisoner, was driven to the necessity of violently entering the London Coffee House, Ludgate Hill, where Mr. Dallimore, the proprietor, stated, he conducted himself with the most unbecoming violence and outrage. The officers and watchmen, however, by this time being pretty numerous, the prisoner was, after a considerable struggle, secured and conveyed to the watchhouse, from thence to the Compter, where his conduct was violent in the extreme.

The residence of the young lady being ascertained, notice was sent to her parents, and her father having soon after arrived at the London Coffee House, she and her sisters were safely conducted home. A number of witnesses were examined upon the subject, all of whom confirmed, in greater or less degree, the violence of the prisoner throughout the whole of these proceedings.

Morning Chronicle, 31 August 1815

SMUTTY AFFAIR. An elopement has, within these few days, taken place from the neighbourhood of Twickenham [west of London], which is at present the topic of conversation among some very respectable families there. A young lady is an only child, and her paramour is a man of colour. *Royal Cornwall Gazette, 4 November 1815*

1816

Parisian Elopement. Lady — L—, daughter of the D— of R—, eloped from her family on Sunday morning, and married Gen. M—tl—nd. The D—ss, her mother, manifested the highest displeasure; but the D— of W—n having volunteered to reconcile the parties, all difficulties were smoothed down, and by dinner-time they met together as a united family.

Royal Gazette of Jamaica, 9 March 1816

Lady Sarah Lennox, daughter of Charles Lennox, 4th Duke of Richmond and Lennox, eloped with Peregrine Maitland, possibly because her father found the age difference between them unacceptable – Sarah was twenty-three to Maitland's thirty-eight – or because she was expected to make a better match. The Duke of Wellington, at whose headquarters in Paris the couple married, was said to have mediated a truce.

1817

The family of a respectable merchant residing in the neighbourhood of Kennington [Surrey] were on Friday morning thrown into a state of considerable alarm. On assembling at the breakfast table it was discovered that Miss M—, the sister of the lady of the mansion, was missing. A search was immediately set on foot; and, after some time, it was ascertained that the lady, who is neither young nor beautiful, but who possesses an independent fortune of £8000 had quitted the house under the influence of the blind god, at the early hour of six in the morning, and having been met at the garden-gate by one of her brother-in-law's clerks, a dashing youth of 21, whose person is his only patrimony, she was by him handed into a chaise and four, which was in waiting near at hand, and they immediately set off in pursuit of connubial happiness with all the speed which four post-horses could give to them. The anxieties of the family, on account of the lady, were quieted by a letter received from her in the course of the evening of Friday, in which she held out to them hopes of a speedy return to town: and assured them, she was convinced the step she had taken would secure her own felicity for life, and add to the happiness of the family.

Bury and Norwich Post, 2 April 1817

Miss G. [Maria Glenn], a young West Indian [that is, born on the island of St. Vincent] lady of 17, entitled to a very large property on her coming of age, and who is a ward of chancery, eloped on Monday last with Mr. J.B. [James Bowditch], a young man of about 24 years of age, residing with his mother, who keeps a farm at Holway Green, near this town [Taunton, Somerset]. Miss G. lives with her guardian in this town, who is a respectable provincial barrister, and whose children, as well as Miss G. having the whooping cough, it was thought advisable to send them from home for change of air. Mrs. B.'s house at Holway Green was selected for this purpose, and here the attachment originated, which led to the young lady's elopement.

The parties travelled with considerable expedition into Dorsetshire, and stopped at the house of a relative of Mrs. B.'s, intending to proceed to London. A marriage licence had been duly provided, but the place of their retreat having been discovered, a respectable gentleman of this town was dispatched to the spot, who brought off this would-be Pastorella [young shepherdess], without her Strephon [male lover], in a chaise and four, on Tuesday afternoon, and lodged her with her friends, like a deposit in our Savings Bank, to be reserved until a few more years have improved the amount of her fortune and the value of her affections. The lady professes the most enthusiastic and inviolable attachment to the object of her choice, but she wants four years to be of age; and some slanderers of the 'belle passion' have affirmed (though on the part of the ladies we protest against heresy) that the flame of love's torch is very apt to fade, and become extinguished in such an intolerable period. We are informed that during their absence, the conduct of the parties was irreproachable. *Taunton Courier, 25 September 1817*

This story is told in detail in my book The Disappearance of Maria Glenn. Maria claimed she was taken from her uncle's home during the night by members of the Bowditch family who had bullied her into silence about the plan. The incident resulted in the prosecution of ten people for conspiracy and, after that, countersuits against Maria. The Taunton Courier article contains numerous deliberate inaccuracies.

1818

A letter from Boulogne-sur-Mer states, that on Tuesday se'ennight, between the hours of ten and eleven o'clock in the forenoon, notwithstanding the vigilance of the French police, who, it was understood, were directed to be on the alert, to prevent the circumstance being carried into effect, a gallant young Officer of the Dragoon Guards, cantoned in the vicinity of Calais, eloped with a lovely and accomplished young lady, niece to a worthy Baronet well known in the west of England: both in the disguise of domestics to some friends who accompanied them. On the following morning they were seen prosecuting their journey to the north of England, and probably ere this the indissoluble knot is tied. *Exeter Flying Post, 22 January 1818*

Late on Friday night last, a young lady, daughter of a respectable inhabitant, eloped from Tewkesbury [Gloucestershire], in a post chaise, with a young widower (one of her father's servants, who buried his wife only a few weeks since), on a matrimonial excursion; but the news having reached the father's ears long after he had retired to rest, he arose and pursued them with such alacrity in a chaise and four, that he overtook them at Worcester, and brought the fair fugitive back to her family the next morning.

Manchester Mercury, 24 November 1818

1819

An elopement took place lately at Carmarthen [South Wales], of a young lady, 17 years of age, with a young chemist and druggist. While her mother was engaged in entertaining some friends, one evening, at a tea and card party, they took the opportunity of proceeding in a post-chaise to Trecastle, 36 miles off, where they ordered two beds; but before they rose in the morning her mother and a friend arrived, and after an interview, Miss was prevailed on to return, upon the promise being made her that she should marry her *dear Henry*, which being agreed to, the mother, the daughter and the friend, returned home. The lover returned by the coach. A fortnight after their wishes were gratified.

Hampshire Chronicle, 4 January 1819

1820

Tuesday, a beautiful young lady, seventeen years of age, eloped with the son of her father's head clerk, twenty years of age, who had just returned home from sea. Her father, Mr. A., a respectable and opulent brewer, residing in Norwich, traced the fugitives to London. He gave information at the Police Office, Hatton-garden, and William Read, jun. was deputed to assist Mr. A. in the inquiry. They proceeded to Doctors' Commons [a civil law court], where they learned that the young man had just taken out a license on affidavit, that the young lady was above twenty-one years of age, and that they were to be married next morning (Friday last), at the parish church of St. Andrew, Holborn. Mr. A. on representing that his daughter was a child under age, procured an order to the clergyman to forbid the marriage. He lost no time in presenting the order, and on Friday morning he took his station facing the church, on Holborn-hill, watching the arrival of the fugitives. Mr. A. did not wait long before he observed the youth, in company with another gentleman, and gave him in charge to the street keeper, who took him in custody. The young lady, who was disguised in a black bonnet and borrowed clothes, walked on the opposite side of the street in company with the gentlewoman in whose house she lodged, seeing her father and what followed, she fled, unperceived. Mr. A. promised Read a large reward if he could recover his lost child in the course of the day, and Read fortunately discovered her about four o'clock the same afternoon, in the neighbourhood of the Coburg Theatre [now known as the Old Vic, in Lambeth]. By the persuasion of the lady of the house and the officer, she dressed herself in her own clothes and returned to her father, who received her with all paternal affection, and took her under his own care. The disappointed youth was then liberated.

Morning Chronicle, 11 September 1820

A duel was bought on Saturday, in a field at Child's-hill, near Hampstead, between Mr. M—–, a young gentleman studying anatomy, and a Mr. C—–g, in consequence of the former having attempted to elope with the sister of the latter. The parties fired without effect, and after re-loading an adjustment of the affair was attempted in vain. In the second fire Mr. C. was wounded above the hip, and there are scarcely any hopes of his recovery.

Royal Cornwall Gazette, 2 December 1820

1821

Miss H—–, a young lady of great accomplishments, the daughter of a wealthy citizen, eloped from the house of her aunt, in New Road [now Euston Road], St. Pancras, where she was on a visit, on Sunday morning last, with a dancing master. The affair was not discovered until the breakfast hour, when it was found that she had taken her trunk with her. Handbills led to a trace of the fugitives on Monday morning, at Buntingford, [Hertfordshire], where they were found. The lady, who is 21 years of age, was brought back by her brother, and the gallant, who is turned 40, received a caning from the brother's hands.

Morning Chronicle, 23 May 1821

The town of Gravesend [in Kent] was last week the scene of much bustle, in consequence of an Elopement which look place between an officer, said to be in the Guards, and the daughter of a general. An attachment had subsisted for some time between the parties, their union, however, was opposed by the family of the young lady, who determined to prevent it, by sending her to the East Indies. She was put on board a vessel lying off Gravesend, in company with her father and brothers, and was to have sailed on the following day. Her lover by some means gained information of her situation, and hastened to the scene of action with a determination of making an effort to recover his fair one. He succeeded in conveying a request to her that she would hold herself in readiness to escape, if a boat with certain marks should approach the ship. About seven in the evening he started in disguise, with four dexterous rowers, and as he neared the ship, he perceived with his glass [telescope] the lady walking the deck: he boldly approached, and in an instant the fair damsel, in the presence of father and brothers, who had not the slightest suspicion that such a *coup de main* was in contemplation, slipped down the side of the vessel, and was carried off. They were quickly pursued to Gravesend, where they were delayed in procuring post horses, and fortune once more appeared to be against them. The father and brothers accidentally entered the very house where the fugitives were, and insisted that the lady should be given up. By this time the circumstances of the case were all known in the town, and it was intimated to the Captain, by some of the resident watermen, who are always upon the look-out for what they term "a lark," that when all was ready he should not be prevented from carrying off the object of his wishes. A chaise and four was soon procured, when a determined scuffle took place; might, however, overcame right, and again had the friends the mortification of seeing the lady fly before their faces. They were quickly followed to London, and traced as far as Charing-cross, where no further clue could be gained to guide pursuit. The lady is young, and of very interesting appearance. Her lover was well supplied with money.

Royal Cornwall Gazette, 18 August 1821

1822

About a fortnight since a young man, of the name of HORATIO REEVES, a journeyman chemist of Exeter, eloped from that place with a young Lady, of the name DRUSILLA HILL, alias STREET, who is a Ward in Chancery, and said to possess a fortune of thirty thousand pounds. She is but fifteen years and six months old, although she has the appearance of being considerably older.

HORATIO REEVES is about 25 years of age. On their elopement from Exeter being discovered, every possible exertion was made in pursuit of them. They were traced to Bristol, and [said] to have left that place by the Regulator coach for London, where they arrived on Monday the 1st instant, when all trace of them ceased; but every possible exertion was made by the agents in London to the parties interested, to prevent their being married, describing their persons, and cautioning clergymen against marrying them. No trace could be made till Wednesday night, when Bishop the Bow-street officer discovered them at a lodging in Hoxton [east London], where he secured them both, and conveyed them to a house in the neighbourhood of Bow-street, where he detained them during the night.

Yesterday they underwent an examination before the Attornies and Agents engaged in the pursuit, when after Horatio Reeves had been served with a process from the Court of Chancery, and a piece of cloth returned to him, which he had made the young Lady a present of, he was not detained any longer, and sent away in a hackney coach, taking with him his luggage; he was in tears, and apparently in great distraction of mind. Miss Hill was sent back to Exeter, under the care of Bishop the officer.

Morning Post, 12 July 1822

At the Guildhall, Exeter, on Friday, a serious charge was made before the Right Worshipful the Mayor, against Mrs. Street, mother of Drusilla Street, of an attempt to poison her husband, previous to the elopement, of which the public has lately heard so much. John Bennet, shoemaker, in St. Sidwell's, deposed, that he called on the defendant to borrow 7*s* [seven shillings].

She said she could put him in the way to get £20; he asked

how, and she replied, "By poisoning my rogue of a husband." She showed him some white stuff, mixed up in a tea cup, which she said was arsenic she had got to poison rats with, but she did not think it was strong enough, and gave him money to go to Mr. Reeves to buy some more. He went and asked for arsenic to poison rats; Mr. Reeves told him nux vomica was better, and gave him some. While his deposition was making, the defendant cried bitterly, and exclaimed – "Lord have mercy upon me!"

A conversation then took place between the counsel and attornies on the amount of bail necessary. Mr. Street said he feared he would be obliged to leave Exeter, to be safe from his wife. Mrs. Street (in great agony) – "I won't injure him – I won't injure him a pin's point!" It was ultimately agreed to take the bail of two persons in £200 each, for her appearance at the sessions to answer the charge. *Hampshire Chronicle, 12 August 1822*

Mr. Horatio Reeves, some time since committed to the Fleet, for an attempt to marry Miss Drusilla Street, a ward in Chancery, was released from confinement on Monday, after his case had been heard before the Chancellor.

Norfolk Chronicle, 23 November 1822

MARRIED. Mr Horatio Reeves, druggist, to Miss Drusilla Street, both of Exeter. These are the parties who excited so much interest in 1822, when the lady was made a ward in chancery.

Bath Chronicle and Weekly Gazette, 15 May 1828

In the 1861 census, Horatio, aged 60, a 'retired druggist', and Drusilla, 54, were recorded as living in Withycombe Raleigh, Devon with a female lodger. I have not been able to find out what happened in the case against Drusilla Street's mother.

1823

On Saturday last considerable sensation was produced in the north-east corner of this county, by the elopement of a young Lady scarcely out of her teens, with a Gentleman on the verge of 50. She had been on a visit in the neighbourhood of Sunderland [north-east England], and, being expected home that evening, the coach was met on the road by the father, who was told that she had quitted it about half an hour before, on pretence of indisposition, and was observed to step into a post chaise, which immediately drove off in the direction of Newcastle. The mother of the Lady, suspecting who the Gentleman was, lost no time in pursuing, and, on her arrival in Newcastle, was informed that the Gentleman she suspected was then in bed at the house of his brother. Insisting on an interview, he acknowledged her suspicions to be well founded, but refused to say whither the lady had retired. The morning, however, brought this secret to light, when she was discovered to be at the Three Indian Kings [an inn], where she had slept the preceding night. It is said, though from the respectability of the parties we cannot think it probable, that on their arrival at Newcastle it was found that no fund had been provided for the prosecution of their journey to Gretna; the gentleman having depended upon the lady, and the lady, of course, upon the gentleman, for supplying the needful. This being an obstacle not to be surmounted, the parties separated for the night, and the lady being discovered, as we have stated, next morning, was compelled, with great and manifold, reluctance, to accompany her mother to C——. (*Durham Chronicle.*)

Morning Post, 27 August 1823

A few days ago a young Lady, 25 years of age, and 27 inches in height, took a fancy to a strapping young fellow in this neighbourhood, and eloped with him, first taking eighty guineas from her father's desk. The fugitives were, however, pursued, taken, and comfortably lodged in the gaol of this town. The wags, alluding to the stature of the fair one, combined with other matters, say she will be made a *show* of at the next Assizes. — (*Carlow Paper*).

Morning Post, 17 October 1823

In the Court of Chancery, on Wednesday, an application was made to the Lord Chancellor, in the case of a young lady of the

FIG.34 A False Alarm on the Road to Gretna 'tis only the Mail! by Richard Gilson Reeve (1838) after Charles B. Newhouse. A fugitive bride fears that her relatives have caught up with her on the road to Gretna. See also pages 177 and 193.
Yale Center for British Art, Paul Mellon Collection. B1985.36.744

name of [Alice] Macdonald, a ward of the Court, who had eloped from a seminary in North Wales, and had married the Rev. James James, a curate in the neighbourhood of the school. The Rev. gentleman had gone abroad, and placed the lady once more in the protection of her guardian. The Lord Chancellor was inclined to consider the affair as a conspiracy to obtain the fortune of the young lady; and directed that she should be placed in a proper seminary, and the validity and circumstances of the marriage would be considered the next Seal Day.

Bath Chronicle and Weekly Gazette, 25 December 1823

COURT OF CHANCERY. —Dec. 17. WARD OF THE COURT. DAVID TENANT AND OTHERS V. SARAH VAUGHAN. Mr. HART stated, that the application he was about to make to his Lordship, was one of a pressing nature, and respected a Ward of the Court, who had been married by a Clergyman in Wales. The infant, Alice Macdonald was the illegitimate daughter of a Mr. Macdonald, who had died testate, and the daughter had become possessed of property to a very large amount, left to her by the testator. The present petitioners had been appointed guardians of the infant, and had placed this young lady at a house in Wales, for the instruction of her mind.

It appeared that the infant being then of a very tender age, was run away with from school, by a Clergyman of the name of James James, residing in the neighbourhood. When these circumstances occurred some time ago, an application was made to the Court by the petitioners, and it was represented that the young lady had been taken away, and that it was not known where she was gone to. On the 3d July, the Court, upon this statement of facts, directed an order to restrain Mr. James James from contracting marriage with the infant, and to restrain all other persons from procuring marriage with her until further order.

The Learned Counsel stated, that it had now been discovered, and the fact was proved by affidavit, confirmed by the certificate of marriage, that the infant and James James were married some days after the order was pronounced. The order had not been personally served on the parties previous to the marriage, and it had not been discovered whither they had gone. The certificate, a copy of which he now held in his hand, contained a falsehood (at the least a legal falsehood) upon the face of it. It was as follows:

"James James, aged 25, and Alice Macdonald, aged 18, were married in this Church by banns with consent of parents, this 13th July, in the year of our Lord, 1823. (Signed) " T. EVANS."

Mr. HART proceeded to state, that the Rev. T. Evans appeared to be the Parish Minister, who had married the parties. There were added to the certificate the names of three attesting witnesses. It appeared that Mr. John James, the brother of the clergyman who had run away with the Ward, was privy to the transaction; and it was also in evidence, that Mr. James James had left the young lady, and had gone over to the Continent...

Although it was stated in the certificate that the young lady was 18 years of age, yet she was in fact only sixteen years old, and perhaps a reference to the Master therefore for this purpose would be the most preferable course. Upon this order being made, the rest of the petition might stand over, with liberty to serve the parties with notice, to enable them to appear before the Court.

The LORD CHANCELLOR: Let the parties be served with a copy of the petition, and let it stand over till the second seal after the Christmas vacation, and in the meantime take the reference to the Master. Mr. ROUPELL doubted whether the instructions to the Master should not proceed further, and whether he ought not to be directed to inquire with respect to the marriage of the parties. It appeared that the husband of the lady had left her, and had gone abroad.

The LORD CHANCELLOR: I cannot consider that the parties are married, until the fact is satisfactorily proved to me; and I shall be glad to see the person who will propose to prove it to me. Mr. HART thought that all that could now be done would be to take the order of reference to the Master, as his Lordship had been pleased to give it.

The LORD CHANCELLOR: With respect to the marriage of these persons, I can only say, that if Mr. Evans has been unfortunate enough to marry the Ward of the Court, he has been guilty of a contempt of Court. That gentleman might be ignorant at the time that she was a Ward of the Court, and that certainly would be a circumstance to be considered. I have, however, no doubt but that that gentleman will have no difficulty in informing the Court how it happened that he had entered it as a marriage "by banns with consent of the parents." There must have been some persons who personated the parents. If so, it may turn out to be a foul conspiracy.

The order of reference to the Master was then taken, and a copy of the Petition was directed to be served upon the parties.

Morning Chronicle, 18 December 1823

The Rev. James James, aged twenty-five, and Alice MacDonald, who declared herself to be eighteen, married in the parish church at Moughtrey in Montgomeryshire on 13 July 1823. The case continued in the Court of Chancery into 1824. I have not been able to discover the outcome.

1824

ELOPEMENT. A post chaise drove up to the Town-hall police office on Tuesday, from which alighted Captain M—, a gentleman residing near Farningham [Kent], and the landlord of the Black Bull in that town, and inquired for Kinsey, the officer, the parties being in pursuit of the eldest daughter of the Captain, who had eloped with her father's coachman, George. That officer immediately dispatched his beagles, and in less than two hours the fugitives were intruded upon in the act of sitting down to dinner, at the public-house known by the sign of "The World turned upside down," (strange coincidence) in the Kent road.

The enamoured pair were directly brought to the Justice-room, and intelligence forwarded to the Captain, who immediately accompanied the messenger back. A scene ensured that excited commiseration for the misplaced attachment of the young lady, who is in her 18th year, petite, of wax-like beauty, and who accompanied her parent with reluctance, casting many a lingering look behind. The Lady's family, we understand, is allied to Nobility, and her father high in East India affairs. — *Morning Papers.*

The Examiner, 18 July 1824

1825

Thursday morning some children, who were rambling through the fields near Kingston-upon-Thames [Surrey] in search of blackberries, discovered in a hedge a young woman almost insensible, and nearly destitute of clothing; assistance was immediately procured, fortunately in time to save the fleeting life of the miserable girl, who was then reduced to the last state of famine. When sufficiently recovered, she gave the following melancholy history of herself:— Her parents were in a respectable sphere of life, residing at Gosport [Hampshire]. While on a visit at Portsmouth, at a friend's house, she became acquainted with young gentleman, who, under the specious show of affection and promise of marriage, induced her to elope with him; but on her arrival in the metropolis, she was abandoned by her heartless seducer. She had determined to return to her friends, and had proceeded her way homewards as far as Kingston-upon-Thames, when her resources failed; and being unable to procure the common necessaries of life, she wandered into the fields, where she subsisted on wild berries for three days, when nature being exhausted, she lost all firmness mind, and awaited death. She is an extremely handsome girl, only 18 years of age.

Bath Chronicle and Weekly Gazette, 29 September 1825

Possibly an apocryphal story. See also page 144.

1826

An elopement took place in the vicinity of Blackheath [south of London], on Wednesday. The parties were Miss T——l, the daughter of a retired tradesman, aged 22, and Mr. P——n, who was admitted to the table of the family on terms of friendship. The parties were pursued to Canterbury, having gone the Maidstone road to avoid detection. The fugitives were surprised at a small inn, and the lady was brought home by her father and brother, with much reluctance. They were to have been married at Ashford, the next day. *Worcester Journal, 26 January 1826*

FIG.35 One Mile from Gretna, Our Governor in Sight — with a screw loose! by Richard Gilson Reeve (1836) after Charles B. Newhouse. The runaway couple are relieved to see that their pursuers' coach has broken down. See also pages 177 and 188.
Yale Center for British Art, Paul Mellon Collection. B1985.36.743

On Friday last, Moses Benjamin [Baruch] Lousada, Esq. of Finsbury-square, a [Jewish] gentleman well known, and highly respected, as a member of the Stock Exchange, put a period to his existence; having been for several days previously in a state of distraction, caused by disappointment, chiefly of a domestic nature. During the last fortnight it was observed by his friends that he laboured under an extraordinary depression of spirits, which was attributed to some losses which he sustained in common with other respectable Stock brokers, by the recent failures. His eldest daughter eloped about a fortnight ago with one of his clerks, a circumstance which appeared, it is said, nearly to drive him frantic. The marriage was subsequently announced in the newspapers, after the parties returned from Gretna Green. "In Scotland, Charles, second son of B. Kendrick [sic], Esq. to Bella, eldest daughter of M.B. Lousada, Esq. of Finsbury-square." On Friday last, a little before the hour of twelve o'clock, Mr. Lousada went to Badler's Warm Baths, St. Mary-axe, and ordered a bath to be prepared. The servant had left him little more than a quarter of an hour, when he committed the act which deprived him of existence. *Morning Chronicle, 27 February 1826*

The parish register at the church of St. Luke in Finsbury, states that on 26 April 1825 [sic — an error for 1826], Charles Kenrick married Bella Kenrick 'having heretofore married to each other on the twenty first day of November 1825 at Gretna Green... with the consent of Bella Baruch Lousada, widow, the natural and lawful mother of the said Bella Kenrick'.

An elopement took place here [Bath] a few days ago, which has caused some conversation. A young tradesman paid his addresses to the daughter of a neighbour, but the father objected to the match. In consequence, it was settled by the lovers, that the young lady should set out privately for London, accompanied by her maid, and that the lover should follow after and marry her. The lady did so; but when her father found that his daughter was gone, he went to her intended husband, and threatened him with vengeance if he did not confess whither she had fled. The ardent lover found himself somewhat cooled by this peremptory order, and confessed where the object of his choice was sojourning — viz., at the Swan-with-two-Necks [a coaching inn in the City]. The enraged father immediately procured a post-chaise and set out for town, where, on his arrival, he found that his daughter had taken a private lodging. After considerable difficulty, however, he discovered her, brought her back to Bath, and it is now his intention to place her without the reach of her constant swain. —*Bath Journal.* *Exeter Flying Post, 27 April 1826*

The name of the young lady from Bath, who eloped to Gretna Green with Mr. Stapleton [Staplyton], as stated in our last number, was Johnson. When they drove up to the Crown Inn, Penrith, an elderly gentleman stepped out the house, and welcomed their arrival with great cordiality, and they all retired to a parlour with apparent satisfaction. But there the scene changed for the old gentleman, who was the father to the bridegroom, made the lady a prisoner, and declared his intention of staying the proceedings. The young gentleman, however, privately ordered horses to his carriage, and upon signal being given that "all was right," he made an overwhelming attack upon his old dad, who now by the chance of war, became a prisoner in his turn: the waiter dexterously conducted the young lady to the carriage; the bridegroom then let go his prisoner, and made a kind of hop-step-and-jump into the vehicle also, but closely pursued by his father; and here the affair became truly interesting: the son shouting to the post-boys to "go on," and the father vociferating counter orders; but the lads cracked their whips, and away flew four as good horses as ever winged happy lovers to the temple of Hymen. The old gentleman immediately went to a magistrate and obtained warrant against his son for an assault, took a constable with him, and set off with other four horses in pursuit, first offering a hundred guineas reward, if his son were apprehended before he crossed the border. It appeared, however, in the sequel, that the youthful pair attained the object of their wishes, and also soothed the angry passions of the father; for, on the following day, they all returned together in seeming good humour, while the emblem of innocence gaily floated in the breeze, and they pursued their journey homeward, in the splendid carriage of the old gentleman, who took quiet possession of the plain post chariot of his son. The old gentleman is Martin Stapleton, Esq. of York, formerly well known the medical world as Dr. Bree, who some years ago changed his name on coming into possession of an estate. The young lady, as we have said, was Miss Johnson of Bath, and ward to the senior Mr. Stapleton.

Chester Chronicle, 26 May 1826

Lucy Margaretta Seaman Johnson, aged fifteen, and 21-year-old Bryan Staplyton (or Bree) were married at Gretna Green on 9 May 1826 and ten weeks later married again at St. Marylebone parish church in London. Lucy was a daughter of Charles Johnson, the Prebendary of Wales.

1827

ELOPEMENT.—We are informed that an occurrence of this kind took place from Loughborough, a few days ago. The young lady, only fifteen years of age, is the daughter of a respectable inhabitant of that place, and the gay Lothario, no less a personage than a Mr. H., a widower with three children, lately belonging to a company of comedians, but who a short time ago left that company, and has since remained at lodgings in the town, in order, no doubt, to carry his designs more effectually into execution. It appears that he had so far succeeded with the young lady, as to induce her to elope with him to London and had actually proceeded by coach as far as Kibworth [Leicestershire], on their way, where fortunately for the lady, they were overtaken by her brother, when a regular fight and rescue ensued. *Pottery Gazette* *Morning Chronicle, 27 February 1827*

An elopement which has caused the greatest surprise in the towns of Wells and Taunton [Somerset], and which from the secret and romantic manner in which it was conducted, and the complete success with which it was attended, rivals the fictions of our best novelists, took place at one o'clock on Friday morning. The Lady was the only child of a Gentleman of fortune, and the fortunate and favoured lover the fourth son of another respectable Gentleman. Secure in the favour of the fair object of his wishes, the lover happy, posted from London, and hovered near the spot which contained his destined bride, till the wished for moment arrived, when in the still hour of night, "*The bell then beating one*," attended by a gallant Captain, a faithful friend, he placed himself beneath the Lady's window — the concerted signal was given and answered — the ladder placed to the wall, the Lady appeared, and descending safely into the lover's arms, was supported by him to a chaise and four in waiting near the spot, and

"They are off — they are gone, over hedge, bush, and bar,"
"They'll have swift steeds that follow, quoth young Lochinvar."

One moment only of anxious suspense attended their flight when the Lady descended from the window, and, at the very instant of departure, a young Gentleman who was attached to the Lady, but who had been rejected, returning from a party "hot with the Tuscan grape," passed the flying lovers; but he gazed, only at the window, sighed, and warbled "*Cherry ripe*." Ill-fated swain, while his passion was thus blighted in the bud.

Thus disappointed, the young Gentleman, in a rage, like *Rodrigo*, flew to the father's door and alarmed the house, when all Taunton was in an uproar. A chaise and four was immediately dispatched in pursuit, containing three Gentlemen, one of whom was the unfortunate young man.

The happy couple reached London in safety, and were immediately married in the presence of a mutual friend, who had prepared for their arrival. *Morning Post, 25 August 1827*

This story may be apocryphal. I can find no trace of it in West Country newspapers. 'They are off…' has been misquoted from Lady Heron's Song in Walter Scott's 1808 historical romance poem Marmion: A Tale of Flodden Field (1808).

This town [Brighton] has just been the scene of an elopement or rather of the recovery of a fair damsel, eloped from her friends. A young lady, about 23 years of age, and of great personal beauty, arrived on Thursday last, by the London coach, at the Pavilion Hotel, where she remained until the next day, when a gentleman made his appearance at the house, and found by the description which was given of the fair fugitive, that the object of his search was safely there. This gentleman was her uncle, and from what has since transpired, we have been enabled to gather the following particulars of the affair. The lady is of a highly respectable family residing at Brixton [Surrey], and had, it seems, formed an attachment with a Frenchman, who was to meet her at Brighton, and for that purpose was expected to arrive by the steam-packet on Saturday from Dieppe.

In order to mislead her friends when she quitted home, she wrote a letter to her mother, in which she declared her intention of proceeding to Dover; and to strengthen this belief, she went by the Brighton coach to town. This she quitted at the Elephant and Castle [Southwark], where she got into the Regent coach, and arrived, as we have stated, at Brighton. Some suspicion being, however, excited that her destination was Brighton, and not Dover, a pursuit was undertaken in that direction; and by a singular coincidence her uncle took his journey by the same coach in which she had herself been conveyed hither.

By the description of the coachman, the uncle was satisfied of the identity of the lady whom he had brought the day before to Brighton, with the object of his search, and went at once to the inn, from which, without delay, he conveyed her by a post-chaise the same evening back to her friends at Brixton. The Frenchman is from 48 to 50 years old. He had formed an intimacy with the lady about eight months ago at a friend's house in England, and since his return to France, a correspondence has been kept up between the parties. Whether he came in the steam-packet on Saturday or not, we have been unable to learn; but another relative of the lady arrived here on that day and went down to the Chain Peer in expectation of meeting him. —*Brighton Gazette.*

London Evening Standard, 8 November 1827

1828

On Tuesday week, Miss Elizabeth Menbinick eloped from her father's house at Tregudick, near Launceton [Cornwall], with Mr. J. Parsons, of Lifton; the fugitives were followed by the Lady's brother, who rested at the same Inn with them at Devonport; the host knowing the business of both parties, sent the brother to Stoke Church, and the happy pair to Stonehouse Chapel, where they were indissolubly united.

Exeter and Plymouth Gazette, 2 August 1828

About a fortnight ago, the London Papers contained an account of a young lady having eloped from her home, with a person in the situation of a menial servant of a performer at the Opera. The parties were subsequently traced to this town [Southampton], and on Thursday, a gentleman came down in pursuit, and with the assistance of Owen [a Bow Street officer], first traced them to a lodging-house in Butcher-row [Whitechapel], and from thence to another on the Castle Hill, where they were, on Friday morning, discovered. The young lady (who is under age) was taken from her *soi-disant* [so-called] husband, and conveyed to London, by the Times coach, leaving the *gentleman*, who is a Spaniard, to bear his bereavement as well as he might. He was at first disposed to be very violent, but a hint at the Alien Act soon reduced him to submission.

Hampshire Telegraph, 3 November 1828

1829

On Saturday morning last, between nine and ten o'clock, a young gentleman, named R., attempted to destroy himself under the following circumstances:—

From some family differences, which it would be improper to publish, Mr. R., who is about nineteen years of age, had resided for the last six months at the house of his uncle, a most respectable solicitor, in Euston place, New-road. During the above period an ardent attachment had taken place between

Mr. R. and his youngest cousin, a young lady of considerable personal attractions and highly accomplished. About a week ago Mr. R. disclosed his views to his uncle, in the hope of obtaining his consent to a marriage with the lady, which was steadfastly rejected by the inexorable parent. While matters were in this unpleasant situation the lover prevailed on his inamorata to elope with him, and render their union indissoluble by a trip to Gretna. After much entreaty the lady consented, and they were on the eve of effecting their escape from the house at an early hour on Friday morning last when [they were] surprised by the father of the lady, who had gained intelligence of their projected flight from a female servant, who had betrayed their secret. The parties were immediately separated, and the following morning the lady was sent off to a relative living at Tiverton, in Devonshire.

The despair and desperation of the lover at this arrangement were so great that a person was specifically appointed to attend on him by his uncle, to prevent any fatal consequences. Appearing somewhat composed on Saturday morning he said to the attendant, before he got up, "Hand me a small smelling-bottle you will find behind the glass on the toilet table." The attendant, not suspecting the least danger, did as he was desired, when Mr. R. emptied the contents, which proved to be laudanum. Two medical gentlemen, named L'Estrange and Lambert, who reside in the neighbourhood, were instantly called in, and, by the prompt application of the stomach-pump, fortunately succeeded in emptying the stomach of the narcotic poison, and saving the young gentleman's life. *London Evening Standard, 8 June 1829*

Yesterday information was sent to Sir Richard Birnie, at Bow-street, informing him that a young lady, the daughter of Lady Brickenden, named Frances Ann Iberton [sic] Brickenden, had suddenly disappeared from the residence of her parents, in Park-place, Hyde-park; and the assistance of the Police was requested, to aid in discovering the young lady's retreat. It appears that the young lady has for some time favoured the addresses of John Clayton Cowell, Esq., a Lieutenant in the Army, who has resided at the Bedford Hotel, Covent-garden. The relatives of the young lady were opposed to the match; and some time ago, for the purpose of breaking off the intimacy between the young lady and the Gallant Officer, she was taken to France, and resided there for a considerable period. Time, however did not obliterate from her heart the deep impressions which had been made by her lover, & on her return to England the Officer contrived to inform her of his readiness to carry her off by a *coup de main*, and to convey her to that country where the nuptial tie is formed without the delay and suspense to lovers occasioned by obtaining a license or the publication of banns.

The young lady, about one o'clock yesterday, left the drawing-room, under the pretext of going to dress for dinner. She had retired to her room about two hours before her absence occasioned any observation, and on a servant being sent to ascertain the cause, he discovered that the room-window was open, and the bird had flown.

It is supposed that she made her exit through the window, and proceeded along the balcony, and entered the window of an adjoining house, which was unoccupied; and her lover there received her, and, without doubt, lost no time in proceeding with her to the North. Inquiry was made after the Lieutenant, at the Bedford Hotel, and it appeared that he had not been there during the day. The mother of the young lady is the daughter of an Irish Earl, and the father is a Clergyman of the Church of England. The elopement has produced an extraordinary sensation in the circles in which the parties moved. The young lady actually left the house without a bonnet, or any apparel except her morning dress.

Morning Chronicle, 13 November 1829

Frances Anne Hester Brickenden was twenty-one when she eloped with John Clayton Cowell, the son of Lieutenant-Colonel Clayton Cowell. They married two days later on 14 November at Christchurch, St. Marylebone. John Clayton Cowell died in 1839 when the ship he was travelling on was lost at sea, leaving Frances with five children.

1830

A few days ago a statement appeared in the Newspapers of the elopement of a young lady from the house of her parents at Shaftesbury [in Dorset], with a foreigner, named Jaunsen, by profession a painter of transparent blinds. Yesterday it was communicated to the Magistrates at Bow-street that the young lady had been restored to her parents. It appears, that with a promise of immediate marriage, in the dead of the night of the 28th of May she contrived to escape from her father's house, and left Shaftesbury with Jaunsen in a chaise and four. They travelled at a great rate, and by a circuitous route reached Andover [in Hampshire], where they stopped at the White Hart Inn, kept by a Mr. Bailey. They remained there several days, during which he paid her every delicate attention, but did not even hint at marriage. One night, after she had retired to her chamber, he entered the apartment, and at once threw off the mask, by declaring that circumstances had occurred which formed an irresistible barrier to their union by marriage at that time, and endeavoured to prevail upon her to allow him at once the privileges of a husband, swearing the most awful oaths that he would fulfil his engagements to her to the very letter as soon as the obstacles he had hinted at were removed. He met with an indignant refusal, and the young lady was about to inform the inmates of the hotel, when he drew a razor from his pocket, bade her be quiet, and then said he would cut his throat open in her presence, unless she compiled with his wishes. The terrified girl still refused; but she became so ill that he was alarmed and left her for that night. On the following morning Mr. Bailey... ventured to question the young lady... and she burst into tears and told him the whole truth... Jaunsen, learning what had passed, suddenly *decamped*, leaving his bill unpaid, and on Friday evening last the young girl was happily restored to her friends. Jaunsen has not since been heard of. He was once confined for a year and a half in Exeter Gaol, for the abduction of a young lady, under somewhat similar circumstances. He looks to be at least ten years younger than he really is.

Morning Chronicle, 24 June 1830

FIG.36 The Assignation by Thomas Rowlandson (1799). A military man leads his lover towards the waiting chaise and pair. A complicit servant lights their way.
Yale Center for British Art, Paul Mellon Collection, Folio A 2018 39

1831

On Sunday last the daughter of a highly respectable Clergyman, not fifty miles from Carmarthen [in South Wales], eloped with an embryo divine [unordained clergyman], and before their friends had concluded their morning devotions the fair fugitive had tied the indissoluble knot. Her father and the rest of the family were on their route to church, when the young lady suddenly pretended to have forgot something, and returned home to get it. The party proceeded unsuspectingly to church, whilst our heroine, having got out of sight, bounded along with lightsome heart, undeterred by hedges and ditches, to an appointed place, where she found her expectant lover with a chaise, ready to convey her to a neighbouring parish church, where they were duly married. On their way to the altar they actually passed the lady's family going church, but they had adopted the necessary precaution of pulling up the blinds, to screen themselves from observation. They had chosen Sunday, it is supposed, from the persuasion that "the better day the better deed." *Carmarthen Journal.*

Enniskillen Chronicle and Erne Packet, 23 June 1831

During the past week the family of Mr. L., who is highly respectable and connected with the law, have been thrown into great alarm by the sudden disappearance of the eldest daughter, a young lady of great accomplishments, under the age of 16. On inquiries being made, it was ascertained that the young lady had eloped with a gallant Captain, who had formed an acquaintance with her during his sojourn at her father's residence. After great exertion they were traced to Woolwich [south-east of London], where they had taken up their residence at a public house; and an application having been made for a warrant, which was granted, the Captain was consigned to "durance vile" [a prison sentence] on a charge of abduction. The principle evidence being wanting, the defendant was remanded and a summons issued for the appearance of the servant of Mr. L. who is said to have been privy to the transaction. *Observer.* *Bombay Gazette, 3 August 1831*

1832

MATRIMONY AND PAUPERISM. A few days ago, an amorous pauper (a widower, and the father of a family, who have for some time past, along with himself, been sheltered under the wing of charity in Caldewgate workhouse [in Carlisle]), evinced to the keeper of that establishment that he was not altogether devoid of the genteel notions belonging to high life, by secretly eloping to Gretna [ten miles away] with a buxom girl, much about his own condition and circumstances in life! Like every other lover, the gallant pauper found that "the course of true love never yet ran smooth." As he knew that he had left behind him those who would be averse to the match, he lost no time in presenting himself and his intended before the "far-famed shrine." Like his betters, too, the pauper had his "pursuers;" for no sooner was the hint given to the master of the workhouse, that he was about to have an "increase" in the number of his inmates, than he, as in duty bound, set out on horse-back, if possible to be at Gretna in time to prevent the marriage. The disappointed pursuer, however, had not gone far till he met with the joyous swain and his happy bride returning; but, alas! their connubial happiness was doomed to be of short duration for though "love may laugh at locksmiths," the urchin has to change his tone whenever he comes in contact with a parish overseer. And so it proved in this instance; for the luckless bridegroom was conveyed before a Magistrate, by whom he was committed to the tread-mill for six weeks — there to enjoy in anticipation, what fate had denied him in reality — the promised joys of his honeymoon! —*Carlisle Patriot.*

Morning Chronicle, 31 January 1832

A few days since, at the close of public business, and the Magistrates of Bow-street being about to retire, a tall, *brisk, hearty* YOUNG Gentleman, apparently about sixty, entered the office in great haste, followed close by a police constable, and addressing the Magistrates, inquiring if any charge had been made before them against a person of the name of

Brown, relative to an elopement, which was to have taken place several days ago.

Mr. Minshull said that he had not heard of any such case.

The Gentleman said that a charge had been preferred before the Magistrates at Marlborough-street, on Saturday last, by the mother of the young lady, who was said to have been carried from a boarding-school by an elderly gentleman, whose name began with Mr. B.

Mr. Minshull,— I really know nothing of the case.

The Gentleman observed that the application had been published in Sunday Papers, and he understood that information had been lodged at this office, and that the mother of the young lady was now in attendance.

Mr. Minshull having ascertained that the mother was not in the office, said he supposed the applicant attended on behalf of the young lady's family.

Applicant,— No, Sir; my name is Brown, and I am the identical Mr. B. mentioned in the newspapers as having seduced the young lady from her school.

Mr. Minshull expressed some surprise, and asked Mr. Brown under what circumstances he appeared before him. Mr. Brown explained that the constable to whom he pointed, had called upon him in the course of the day, and told him that his presence was required at Bow-street, to answer the charge of having carried off the young lady in question.

Mr. Minshull inquired her name. Mr. Brown stated that she was the daughter of the late Dr. Milner, a Protestant divine, who died about three months ago, while confined for debt, in Horsham gaol. He knew him well, having been a lodger in his house. The young lady now present had eloped from school and was now living under his roof.

Mr. Minshull— May I ask under what circumstances she came under your protection.

Mr. Brown said that he was quite willing to enter into any explanation respecting the voting lady which the Magistrates might think fit to require. He then went on to state that after she ran away from the school of Mrs. Field, near Great Marlow [in Essex], he succeeded in tracing her to Newington-causeway [in Southwark], and, her father being dead, took her to his own residence, where she had been for the last six months.

Mr. Minshull— Pray, Sir, are you a married man.

Mr. Brown replied that he was a bachelor, but kept a housekeeper, who was a most respectable woman.

Mr. Minshull, addressing the young lady, asked her if she had any charge to prefer against Mr. Brown, or had any complaint to make of his conduct towards her. Miss Milner replied, certainly not. He had treated her like a father.

Mr. Minshull— Did never take improper liberties with you?

Miss Milner— Oh dear! No Sir; I will take my oath of that.

Mr. Minshull then asked the constable upon whose information, or by whose direction he had acted?

The constable replied that he had read the statement in the papers, and, as he was on his duty that morning, in Southwark, a woman told him that the gentleman who had eloped with the young lady, as stated in the Police report, was living in Prospect-place, St. George's-road. He went to the house described, by direction of his inspector, and there found Mr. Brown and the young lady.

Mr. Brown said the statement in the papers was quite untrue. He never carried off the young lady, and all he did was give her the protection of his house, as she did not wish live with her mother.

Mr. Minshull observed that, in his opinion, the young lady ought to be placed under the protection of her mother, who was her natural guardian.

Miss Milner replied that she would prefer living with Mr. Brown.

Mr. Minshull— I must say that such a resolution is very extraordinary, and gives an appearance to the case not very pleasant.

Mr. Brown said that Mr. Drummond, the banker, and several persons of the highest respectability, knew that Miss Milner was living with him, and produced a list containing the names of the Duchess of Kent, Lord Eldon, the Bishops of Chichester and Worcester, and others, who had subscribed various sums to the amount of £57 for the benefit of Miss Milner in consideration of her being the daughter of a clergyman, who had died in distressed circumstances.

Mr. Minshull said he scarcely knew how act in the case, and asked the constable if the young lady's mother meant to prefer any charge against Mr. Brown...

Mr. Minshull asked Mr. Brown if he followed any business or profession. Mr. Brown replied that he was independent, and that he was brother to Sir William Brown Cave [Sir William Cave-Browne-Cave, 9th baronet of Stanford].

Mr. Minshull said he did not think it right, under all the circumstances, that the young lady should return to the house of Mr. Brown, and he directed the Clerk write a letter in his name to the clergyman of the parish in which Mrs. Milner resided, informing him of the circumstance in which Miss Milner was placed and requesting him to consult her mother as to her final destination.

The constable said that, from what he could understand the young lady was determined to continue with Mr. Brown.

Miss Milner smiled, and observed that it was certainly her wish to remain where she was.

Constable— I believe Mr. B. means to marry the lady.

Mr. Brown— Ay, that I do, sure enough, sooner than she should live with her mother.

Mr. Minshull— And what says the young lady.

Miss Milner— I am quite agreeable—*(laughter)*.

Mr. Brown— And am I.

Miss Milner— 'Tis all settled for next Sunday.

Mr. Minshiill— Do you mean that you are to be married on Sunday Mr. Brown.

Miss Milner— Indeed I do.

Mr. Brown— It is all fixed.— (*A general burst of laughter followed this avowal.*)

Mr. Minshull said that as the affair had taken an unexpected turn, he had nothing further to do with the business, and he told the Clerk that there was no occasion to send the letter.

Mr. Brown & his intended then left the office most *lovingly* together, & thus terminated this very singular scene.

Leicester Journal, 13 July 1832

Thomas Cave Browne and Maria Milner were married at St. George's Church, Old Brompton, on 1 July 1833. According to a report in Freeman's Journal (5 July 1833) this was a second ceremony, 'in consequence of a dispute as to the validity of the first'. Maria, aged twenty-three, died three years later and was buried at Leamington, Warwickshire.

An incorrect account appeared in one or two of the Sunday papers, of the elopement Mr. Horatio Claggett with Miss Letitia [Caroline] Day, the daughter of Mr. Day, of the well known firm of Day and Martin, of High Holborn, on Saturday se'nnight, in consequence of Mr. Day's opposition to their marriage. The following particulars connected with the affair have been obtained from an authentic source:— It has been long known that Mr. Claggett was paying his addresses to the young lady, which were permitted by her father, and it was thought that he was destined to be her husband. However, within these three months Mr. Day, from some anonymous information that he had received, sent for Mr. Claggett, and in the presence of the young lady, refused to give his consent to their union. In vain did Mr. Claggett remonstrate, for Mr. Day was inexorable, and it is said forbid him the house. In this state did matters continue for some time; but, notwithstanding the mandate of the father, the young lady was frequently seen walking and riding with Mr. C. On Saturday se'nnight, she left Harley House, in the New-road [Euston Road], rather early, and never returned. It was at first thought she had gone to her father's seat at Edgeware [north of London], but no tidings could be heard of her there, nor could any trace be had of the retreat of her or Mr. Claggett till Friday last, when it was ascertained that the parties had been married the preceding day, by special licence, at the New Church, Marylebone, almost immediately opposite Mr. Day's residence, yet so private were the movements the parties kept that only a few confidential friends were in the secret. The happy pair and their friends drove off in post-chaises. But their destination is at present unknown to any member of the family. Mr. Claggett is the third son of Mr. Horatio Claggett, of the late well-known firm Claggett and Pratt, the American merchants, in John-street, Minorities [Minories]. He is now in the thirtieth year, and when of age came into possession of a fortune of upwards £20,000. Miss Day is about the same age, and has at her own disposal upwards of £35,000.—*Morning Post.*

Wexford Conservative, 13 October 1832

At the time of his elopement with Letitia Day, Horatio (known as Horace) Claggett was the father of five children with his mistress, Eliza Pyne, who lived at Canterbury Villas, Maida Vale. In 1834 Claggett was declared an insolvent debtor.

1833

An elopement took place two or three days since, attended with more than the usual "hair-breath 'scapes" of such an event. A Captain of the East India Company's Service had become enamoured of the beautiful and accomplished daughter of a wealthy Gentleman residing in the neighbourhood of Camberwell-green [Surrey], and, as usual, the son of Mars, having "told his soft tale, became a thriving wooer," but as "fathers have flinty hearts" no hopes were entertained of his consent, and the loving pair determined on an elopement. At an early hour, therefore, a postchaise was provided, and the Lady, nothing loth, prepared to throw herself into the arms of her adored; but, as "the course of true love never did run smooth," the father was heard in pursuit before she could quit the house. No opportunity of escape offered but to lock him in, which was immediately done. The lovers fled, the father raised the alarm, and the brother of the Lady pursued *en dishabille* [sic, not fully dressed]. They, however, stole a march on their pursuer, and, by taking a circuitous route, contrived, instead of the fatigue and danger of a trip to Gretna, to reach a neighbouring church, where Hymen lit his torch, and the fugitives were united. It is said a reconciliation has since been effected between the parties.

Morning Post, 8 April 1833

The family of Mr. Perkins, the landlord of the large public-house and liquor-shop, called the White Hart, in High-street, Shadwell, [east] London, were thrown into a state of great affliction, on Saturday evening, by the elopement of his youngest daughter, Miss Mary Perkins, a very pretty girl, aged sixteen years.

It appears that, for some time past, an Irish policeman, named Michael Henessey, of the K division, No. 118, had been in the habit of frequently calling at the house, and paying particular attention to Miss Perkins, which had been observed by many, but was not noticed by her parents. On Saturday evening, while serving in the bar, she requested a labourer, named Miller, one of her father's customers, to go to the back of the house and see if Henessey was waiting about, at the same time directing him, if he was there, to return and give a nod, but if he could not see him, he was to shake his head. Miller went out, and observing Henessey, returned and gave the signal as directed, on which Miss Perkins went up stairs under some pretence, and threw a bundle containing her wearing apparel out of a back window, which was caught by Henessey, who made off, and soon afterwards Miss Perkins walked out as she was sometimes in the habit of doing, without any cap or bonnet on. The elder sister, believing that she had gone out to call on a neighbour, took no notice of her absence, until Miller observed that if Mary was gone out she was gone for good; then she communicated the circumstance to the father, who immediately went in search of his daughter, and sent other persons in every direction, but no tidings of the fair fugitive have yet been ascertained; but it is strongly suspected she is secreted in some lodgings hired by the policeman. A parish officer has since waited on Henessey at the station-house of the division, No. 34, Lower Chapman-street, where he has for some time lodged, but he denies all knowledge of Miss Perkins' retreat, and alleges that he was on duty when seen near Mr. Perkins' house, though his beat is half a mile distant. A neighbour saw him receive the bundle which Miss Perkins threw out of the window. Henessey is a very illiterate man, nearly forty years of age. A sergeant of the same division, named Edward Shaw, No. 14, a married man, is suspected of being concerned in the elopement of Miss Perkins, for on Saturday morning Miller was the bearer of a letter to him from her. On Monday Mr. Perkins applied to Shaw for the letter, but he said he had destroyed it, and refused to divulge the contents.

The affair has caused a very extraordinary sensation in the parish of Shadwell, where, since the late murder of Wood the waterman, by a policeman, the police force has been in very bad odour. Another circumstance, though not connected with the affair, is somewhat extraordinary, and is the subject of much conversation. A few hours before the elopement of Miss Perkins, her father received an intimation from one of the superior officers of the police, that complaints had been made that his house was a disorderly one, and that when ostensibly closed for the night, bad characters were re-admitted and allowed to remain, and that an information must be lodged against him if he did not conduct it better in future.

It is but right to state that the White Heart [sic] bears a good character, but it has been for some time very much resorted to by policemen. The White Hart obtained some notoriety during the inquest on Wood, from the fact of its having been the house from which he was violently thrust by one policeman, before he received the fatal blow from another.

Liverpool Standard and General Commercial Advertiser, 4 October 1833

Sixteen-year-old Elizabeth Mary Perkins married Michael Hennessey on 8 October 1833 at St. George in the East, Tower Hamlets, with the consent of her father. The death of the waterman John Peacock Wood took place at the beginning of July while he was being taken in a state of severe inebriation to the police station at Wapping by John Douglas, a police constable.

1834

We are sorry to hear that a gross and serious outrage was commited [sic] on the morning of the 18th inst., in the parish of Clonleigh, about two miles from Lifford [County Donegal,

Ulster]. A man named [Cormick] Tinny, a Roman Catholic, had been for a few months since employed as a servant, by a widow named Wilkie, whose husband, a Presbyterian, a farmer of the most respectable description, died some time since. A younger daughter of the widow, aged only fifteen, was induced by a maid servant, resident with the family, to elope with Tinny on Friday last. Her flight having been immediately discovered, she was pursued by her brothers and friends, and recovered. Such threats were used by Tinny at that time that some young men were induced to keep watch in the widow's house, and prepared with firearms to resist any attack that might be made.

About one o'clock on the morning of the 18th, the house was surrounded by, it is conjectured, fifty or sixty men, many provided with firearms. Previous to the party reaching the house, having met with a neighbour of the Wilkies, named Atcheson, they had the precaution to make him a prisoner in order to prevent him alarming the neighbourhood. Tinny, their leader, demanded admittance, which was refused. Being asked what he wanted, he replied his wages. He was informed that this would be paid, as there was no wish to withhold from him anything to which he had a right. Concession being invariably followed by a new demand, he then required not only the wages, but the girl. He was informed they were prepared to meet an attack, and would fire on them in the King's name if any violence should be used. The house having been then assailed on all sides, the windows broken in with stones, and the muzzles of several guns presented through them, a shot was fired through the door by one of the besieged party, which was immediately returned through the same door, by one of the assailants, and a fine lad, a brother of the girl, desperately wounded. The wounded boy, although only able to use one arm, returned the fire, but without effect – the ball having lodged in the door post. The widow (having put to bed her wounded child) finding further resistance useless, opened the door, and with feelings which may be conceived, but not described, gave her daughter to the ruffian band, which with yells of savage triumph, carried her away. A few hours after this occurrence, a visit not of condolence but of business, was made at the widow's house, by the Rev. Mr.——, R.C.C., and a proposition made by him, that the consent of the family should be given to the union of the parties — which was indignantly refused. Mortified and disappointed, his reverence, meeting with a Protestant neighbour of the Wilkies, assured him "that if he met the couple he would not risk the loss of the *confidence* of his people, by giving any information of the party if he knew where they were." In the course of the same day, informations were lodged before Captain Humphry, J.P., by one of the brothers of the girl. Messrs. Nixon and Dumas, chief constables of police, visited the family and obtained such information as we trust will lead to the apprehension of those concerned, and thereby check the importation of this southern system of brutal violence into the district hereto peaceable. —*Derry Sentinel.*

Kilkenny Moderator, 27 August 1834

The Enniskillin Chronicle and Erne Packet reported on 13 August 1835 that Cormick Tinny had been sentenced at the Donegal Assizes to six months in prison for the attack on Mrs. Wilkie's house. The fate of Miss Wilkie has not been discovered.

1835

One of these little amusing clandestine love expeditions, was about to take place in this neighbourhood few nights since: a rope ladder had just been attached to the window of the fair one's bedchamber and her admirable little foot placed safely on the outside, when the father, suspecting, from the creaking of the casement, all was not quite right, sallied forth, and snatched away the prize just as the enamoured swain, with unfolded arms, was panting with expectation to receive her. The gentleman, who, we are told, was a hero of the sock and buskin [the symbols of comedy and tragedy], and connected with Penley's Company [The Jonas & Penley Company of Comedians], immediately took flight, — and the fair one in tears was conveyed back to a room, where bolts and bars gave a negative to all further attempts.

Reading Mercury, 28 September 1835

1836

On Friday last a young lady, aged 17, named Chinery, who will in a few years become possessed of very considerable property, eloped from her friends at Bury St. Edmund's [Suffolk], in company with a person named Taneure, whom, as it now appears, she had been most infamously deceived. Taneure, who is somewhat of an Adonis in appearance, was shopman to Mr. Sawden, a linendraper in the Old Kent-road, and has friends at Bury St. Edmund's, where he became acquainted with Miss Chinery, and for three years past amatory correspondence has been carried on between them by letter, unknown to the young lady's friends. Taneure had in the meantime been paying his addresses to another, a very respectable young woman from the county of Sussex, to whom he was married last January, and he afterwards lived apparently on good terms with his wife, with whom he obtained some little property. On Wednesday last, however, he disappeared from his home, and upon inquiry at his employer's, it was found that he had gone out in the morning, and was to have returned in the evening. It has been ascertained that instead of doing so, be hired a horse and chaise, and drove to the neighbourhood of Bury St. Edmund's, where he was joined on the following day by Miss Chinery, who believed her lover to be a single man.

It was ascertained that the fugitives met about three miles from Bury, and started in a chaise towards London; and Mr. Carey, Superintendent of Police in that part of Suffolk, came up by the mail in search of them. He applied to a friend, Mr. Brindley, an Inspector in the Metropolitan Police, who assisted him in his search, and they discovered the residence of Mrs. Taneure, upon whom the intelligence of her husband's treachery and infidelity had a very distressing effect. Taneure himself was met with on Tuesday, and being threatened with detention until he disclosed the residence of the young lady whom he had so infamously seduced from her home, he accompanied the Superintendent to a lodging in which he had placed her, in the neighbourhood of the Kent-road. Miss Chinery, who immediately recognised the Superintendent of Police, seemed agitated at the prospect of separation from her lover, who renewed his protestations of ever-enduring affection. She was startled, however, when mention was made of a deserted wife — and still more so, when Taneure had the heartlessness to assert, in the presence of the police, that when she eloped with him she knew him to be a married man. She indignantly denied it — and this proof of baseness seemed at once to reconcile her to return home. Mr. Carey took her to the Catherine Wheel Inn, Bishopsgate-street, where she slept that night; and yesterday morning she was taken back to her friends in Suffolk. *Morning Advertiser, 21 April 1836*

1837

Much conversation has been occasioned within the last week among the fashionable circles at the west-end of the town by the sudden elopement of a young lady, of considerable personal attractions and large fortune, from the residence of her mother at Kensington, on Wednesday last.

The young lady in question had, until within the last few months, a remarkable penchant for some of the conductors of the omnibuses travelling past her residence, on whom she used most lavishly to heap sterling proofs of her admiration and attachment. The illness and sudden death of her brother, however, worked an alteration in her, and subsequent to his death she was addressed by a gentleman of large property in the county of York, with the sanction of her mother... but Miss —— who is in her 21st year, declared she could not 'abide' him, and on the above morning she got up at daybreak, and having safely locked her mother and the servants in their rooms, double-locked the street door, taking the key with her; she then proceeded along the lanes adjoining Lord Holland's park to Notting-hill, where a more favoured lover, a young gentleman residing in Hampstead, was waiting with a chaise, in which they proceeded to his residence; when, after having partaken of refreshment, they started with post-horses for Gretna, where long previous to this, the 'twain' have been made 'one flesh.'

The young lady has a large property at her own disposal, but

Mrs —'s income does not exceed £100 per annum. *Morning Paper*. (This has very much the air of 'a cock-and-bull' story. [sic]) *Southern Reporter and Cork Commercial Courier, 4 May 1837*

Friday morning the eldest daughter of an auctioner of Eynesbury, near St. Neots [Cambridgeshire], escaped by the front door from her residence, notwithstanding the precaution her mother had taken of sleeping with her, but being quickly pursued, was overtaken, and brought back. She started rather earlier than the time appointed, so that the chaise had not arrived with her admirer (who is also of the "going, going!" fraternity, and residing at St. Neots,) and in her hurry to escape fell down and hurt her wrist. Shortly afterwards her father was going to St. Neots for a surgeon, and on his way he met her admirer, upon whom he inflicted a sound drubbing, the young knight of the hammer offering no resistance. Nothing daunted by the above unsuccessful attempt, the young lady on Sunday morning complained of being unwell, and consequently did not arise at her accustomed hour, but feeling somewhat better about 11, she availed herself of the opportunity (her father being from home, and her mother and one of her sisters at [a] meeting) of fleeing into the arms of her lover, and next morning they were married at St. Neots. —*Cambridge Chronicle*. *Clonmel Herald, 7 June 1837*

NOTES

INTRODUCTION

1 Late sixteenth century: 'to run off,' probably from Middle Dutch (ont)lopen 'run away', from ont- 'away from'.

2 *A Complete Collection of State Trials and Proceedings for High Treason and Other Crimes and Misdemeanors, 1696-1709*, Vol. 5, page 449; Edmund Bennett and Franklin Fiske Heard, *A Selection of Leading Cases in Criminal Law*, Vol. 2. Little, Brown and Co, Boston, 1869. The Ramsay case was reported in *The Reports of Sir Peyton Ventris, Kt., Late One of the Justices of Common Pleas* (1726), Vol. 1, p. 243, E. & R. Nutt and R. Gosling.

3 11 September 1721.

4 27 December 1735.

5 T.C. Hansard (1803), *The Parliamentary History of England, from the Earliest Period to the Year 1803*, Vol. 15, A.D. 1753–1765, p. 45 (Clandestine Marriage Bill, John Bond, 7 May 1753). London: Johnson Reprint Company.

6 *Kentish Gazette*, 15 October 1768.

7 *Morning Chronicle*, 10 November 1809.

8 New game of elopement or A trip to Gretna Green. Designed & invented to enliven the winter evenings of 1820. John Johnson Collection of Printed Emphemera, Bodleian Museum. Games folder (7).

THE BRISTOL ELOPEMENT: CLEMENTINA CLARKE & RICHARD VINING PERRY

9 Clementina, the daughter of John Clarke and Isobel née Ogilvie, was baptised in Keith, Banffshire, Scotland 29 April 1776.

10 More was perhaps the only character in this story who we know to have been an Abolitionist.

11 Richard Vining Perry was baptised at Temple Church, Bristol on 7 April 1765. He was apprenticed to William Blagden, a surgeon, on 20 May 1778.

12 *The Trial of Richard Vining Perry, Esq. for the Forcible Abuction, or Stealing an Heiress, from the Boarding-School of Miss Mills, in the City of Bristol*, a pamphlet published in 1794 and giving a transcript of Perry's trial, with a highly biased introduction (probably written by Perry himself), is available online at Cornell University's Trial Pamphlets collection.

13 *The Times*, 24 March 1791.

14 31 March 1791.

15 'Elopement from Bristol — or too many for the Bristol bumbrusher.' British Museum. 1868,0808.6022. The print was published on 25 March 1791 by W. Holland, No. 50, Oxford Street.

16 31 March 1791.

17 The National Archives of the UK; Kew, Surrey, England; Office of Registry of Colonial Slaves and Slave Compensation Commission: Records; Class: T 71; Piece Number: 145.

18 1 January 1810.

19 George H. Gibbs (1947), *Bristol Postscripts*, Bristol; *The Gentleman's Magazine and Historical Chronicle*, 1813, July–December, p. 403.

HOAX! THE MYSTERY OF THE STOCKWELL ELOPEMENT

20 The building is now two separate addresses, 171 and 173 Clapham Road. F.H.W. Sheppard, ed. (1956), 'Stockwell: Lansdowne Way area and Clapham Road.' *Survey of London*. Vol. 26, Lambeth: Southern Area. London: London County Council, pp. 82–88.

21 The events of the night are taken from *The Standard*, 31 December 1829, 1 January 1830; *The Examiner*, 3 January 1830. The episode was widely reported.

22 An obituary of Robert Hedger (1786–1851) appeared in *The Gentleman's Magazine*, Vol. 36, Aug. 1851, p. 219.

23 'Wm. Catchpool' is listed at 162 Fenchurch Street in *The Post Office London* Directory for 1829.

24 *Englishman*, 3 January 1830.

25 *Weekly Dispatch*, 26 Oct. 1828. The appearance of Charles Price, the prisoner, 'indicated misery and want'.

26 *The Comet*, Vol. 1, No. 3 (3 May 1832), p. 39.

27 Theophila Carlile Campbell (1899). *The Battle of the Press: Life of Robert Carlile*. London: A. & H.B. Bonner, p.197.

LORD THURLOW'S GRIEF: CAROLINE HERVEY & SAMUEL BROWN

28 Edward Thurlow (1731–1806); Polly Hervey was also known as Harvey and sometimes Humphries

29 I am indebted for much of this story to R.J.S. [Richard John Samuel] Stevens (1992). *Recollections of R.J.S. Stevens: An Organist in Georgian London*. Ed., Mark Argent. London: Palgrave Macmillan.

'A MAN OF FASHION': ANN WADE & CHARLES BASELEY

30 *Bury and Norwich Post*, 2 November 1814

31 *London Courier and Evening Gazette*, 27 November 1815; *Northampton Mercury*, 26 August 1815.

32 The clerk of St Saviour's (now Southwark Cathedral) noted in the margin of the ledger: 'The banns of marriage of Ann Wade & Charles Basely [sic] were forbidden in this church by Mr. Thos. Broughton, guardian of the said Ann Wade on Sunday the 30th day of October 1814.' London Metropolitan Archives; London, England; London Church of England Parish Registers; Reference Number: P92/SAV/3074.

33 London Metropolitan Archives; London, England; London Church of England Parish Registers; Reference Number: P89/MRY1/290.

A TRAGICAL DRAMA: AUGUSTA NICHOLSON & JOHN GILES

34 *Hampshire Chronicle*, 13 November 1809.
35 The details appeared in, among others, *Saunders's News-Letter*, 11 November 1809.
36 Widely reported, including in the *Kentish Gazette*, 7 November 1809.
37 *Hampshire Chronicle*, 18 November 1811.

THE SHRIGLEY ABDUCTION: ELLEN TURNER & EDWARD GIBBON WAKEFIELD

38 The details of the abduction have been taken from Edward Wakefield (1827), *The Trial of E. G. W., W. Wakefield and F. Wakefield, Indicted with One E. Thevenot, a Servant, for a Conspiracy, and for the Abduction of Miss E. Turner*. London: John Murray. *Morning Post*, 2 March 1820, *Exeter Flying Post*, 8 March 1821.
39 24 August 1826.

AN IRREGULAR MARRIAGE: ARTHUR ANNESLEY POWELL & JEMIMA NEATE

40 Arthur was among the youngest pupils recorded at Harrow. Information from Joanna Badrock, Harrow School's archivist (2015).
41 HL/PO/PB/1/1789/29G3n108, Deed Poll Office.
42 VH 80/50, Lambeth Palace Library.
43 The Rev. Richard Powley, 'late curate of Carham', died in 1820 in the lunatic asylum near the Baths, Newcastle, where he had been confined for 18 years. *The Monthly Magazine*, Vol. 49, p. 377.
44 *The Gentleman's Magazine: Or, Monthly Intelligencer*, Vol. 88, p. 666.
45 *The Oxford University and City Herald* of 11 March 1809: 'The facts were, that Lord F. and Mr P. dined together with a party on Saturday, at Mr P.'s house, and took plenty of wine; went to the Opera, and afterwards became inebriated at the Mount Street coffee-house; next evening (Sunday) they met at Stevenson's hotel, where Lord Falkland, espying his friend Powell, accosted him with "what, drunk again to-night, Pogey!" Mr. Powell, disliking this mode of being accosted, retorted on his lordship, who instantly snatched a cane from the hands of a gentleman present, and laid it on the shoulders of Mr. Powell. The following morning, Lord Falkland went to Mr. Powell's house, and apologised, by asking that gentleman's pardon, and attributed his rash conduct to inebriation. Mr. Powell observed that he could not accept his lordship's apology, unless made at the hotel, before the persons who were present at the outrage. Lord Falkland would not accede to this proposition; and hence ensued the challenge from Mr. Powell, and the subequent duel at Goldar's-green [Golders Green]; where, according to etiquette, Mr. Powell fired first, and inflicted the mortal wound.' Falkland did not fire back. An inquest returned a verdict of Wilful Murder against some person or persons unknown. No further action was taken.

'THESE FEELINGS RIPENED INTO LOVE': SYDNEY HAMILTON & BENJAMIN BERESFORD

46 Beresford, Benjamin and Grey, James (1782). *A Narrative of Circumstances Attending Mr. Beresford's Marriage with Miss Hamilton.* London (no publisher).
47 11 December 1780 at St. Katharine Cree, Aldgate.
48 I am indebted to the account given in Harold Nicolson's *The Desire to Please: A Story of Hamilton Rowan and the United Irishmen* (1943). London: Constable.
49 They married at the church of St. James, Piccadilly, on 12 November 1781.

THE LADIES OF LLANGOLLEN: ELEANOR BUTLER & SARAH PONSONBY

50 See Elizabeth Mavor, *The Ladies of Llangollen* (1973, London: Penguin); *Hereford Journal*, 28 July 1790; *Chester Courant*, 11 August 1829; *Freeman's Journal*, 12 January 1830.

THE ABDUCTION CLUBS OF IRELAND: GARRET BYRNE, JAMES STRANGE & THE KENNEDY SISTERS

51 John Edward Walsh (1851), *Ireland Sixty Years Ago*. Dublin: J. M'Glashan, p.35.
52 Margery Weiner (1967), *Matters of Felony: A True Tale of 18th Century Ireland.* New York: Atheneum.
53 Weiner, *op. cit.*, p. 95.
54 15 December 1780.
55 Weiner, *op. cit.*, p. 189.
56 Weiner, *op. cit.*, p. 85.
57 Quoted in A.P.W. Malcomson, *Pursuit of the Heiress: Aristocratic Marriage in Ireland 1740–1840*. Belfast: Ulster Historical Foundation. pp. 62–3.

THE MISER'S GRANDDAUGHTER: EMILY ELWES & THOMAS DUFFIELD

58 Marcham Park is now in Oxfordshire but was then in Berkshire.
59 *Bury and Norwich Post*, 14 February 1810.
60 *Leeds Mercury*, 17 February 1810.
61 Bligh, Richard (1829). *New Reports of Cases Heard in the House of Lords: On Appeals and Writs of Error; and decided during the session 1827-8*, Vol. 1. London: Saunders and Benning.

'WE FLY BY NIGHT': MARY BARTON & WILLIAM FIELDS

62 *The European Magazine*, Vol. 49, January–June 1806.
63 *We Fly by Night; or, Long Stories*. Hull Theatre Royal playbill (1808). University of Alberta Libraries.
64 *Hull Advertiser and Exchange Gazette*, 5 December 1812.
65 Mary Ann Burton, daughter of William and Ann Burton was baptised at All Saints, Gainsborough on 29 October 1791.

66 *Hull Advertiser and Exchange Gazette*, 2 January 1813.
67 John Craggs (1817), *Cragg's Guide to Hull: A Description, Historical and Topographical, of the Town, County, and Vicinity of the Town of Kingston-upon-Hull.*
68 *Hull Packet*, 1 February 1814.
69 *Hull Packet*, 5 December 1815.
70 *Stamford Mercury*, 6 January 1826.

'THIS LOVE HATH TURN'D THY BRAIN': RICHARD BRINSLEY SHERIDAN & ELIZABETH LINLEY

71 The quotation in the chapter title is from Sheridan's play *The Critic: Or, A Tragedy Rehearsed: a Farce* (1779), II, 2, in Richard Brinsley Sheridan, *Dramatic Works of Sheridan and Goldsmith. With Goldsmith's Poems* (1836), Vol. 2. p.48.
72 Alicia Le Fanu (1824), *Memoirs of the Life and Writings of Mrs Frances Sheridan.* London: G. & W.B. Whittaker.
73 *Bath Chronicle*, 9 April 1772.
74 *Bath Chronicle*, 7 May 1772.
75 *London Magazine*, September 1772.
76 L. B. Seely (reprinted 1895), *Fanny Burney and her Friends: Select passages from her Diary and other Writings.* London: Seeley & Co. (1779).

'THE LAST SOLACE OF MY LIFE': MARCIA GRANT & BRINSLEY SHERIDAN

77 *Court Journal: Gazette of the Fashionable World*, No. 317, p. 317, 23 May 1835.
78 *Morning Post*, 18 May 1835.
79 6 June 1835.
80 *The Spectator*, No. 360, 23 May 1835, p. 485.
81 This story is told in Diane Atkinson's excellent *The Criminal Conversation of Mrs Norton* (2013, London: Arrow Books).
82 *Court Journal*, 19 September 1835, No. 334, p. 596

INDEX

N

O

P

R

S

T

W

Z

ACKNOWLEDGEMENTS

My heartfelt thanks to contributors Sarah Murden and Joanne Major, my partner Tim Clifford, and designer Caroline Jefford. As ever, the staff at the National Archives, the British Library, the British Newspaper Archive, and various collections around the country, both online and in person have been amazing.

OTHER CARET PRESS PUBLICATIONS

Under Fire: The Blitz Diaries of a Volunteer Ambulance Driver (2021) by Naomi Clifford

Six Essays on Vauxhall Gardens (2021) by David E. Coke

Out of the Shadows: Essays on 18th and 19th Century Women by Naomi Clifford (2022)

These Were Our Sons: Stories from Stockwell War Memorial by Friends of Stockwell War Memorial & Gardens

The 1914 Diary of Dora Lourie by Naomi Clifford (in preparation)

Our print editions books are available to order from bookshops and from Amazon. Our ebooks are on major platforms. Visit our website caretpress.com for details.

CARET PRESS

Caret Press is an independent publishing imprint based in London and established in 2021. We specialise in history, essay collections and historical fiction.

To submit your work for consideration please contact us at info@caretpress

Printed in Great Britain
by Amazon

45421834R00132